AQ2016
AAT FOUNDATION CERTIFICATE IN
ACCOUNTING LEVEL 2

QUESTION BANK

Bookkeeping Transactions

2016 Edition

For assessments from September 2016

First edition June 2016

ISBN 9781 4727 4845 4

British Library Cataloguing-in-Publication Data
A catalogue record for this book is available from the
British Library

Published by

BPP Learning Media Ltd
BPP House, Aldine Place
142-144 Uxbridge Road
London W12 8AA

www.bpp.com/learningmedia

Printed in the United Kingdom by Martins of Berwick

Sea View Works
Spittal
Berwick-Upon-Tweed
TD15 1RS

Your learning materials, published by BPP Learning
Media Ltd, are printed on paper obtained from traceable
sustainable sources.

CONTENTS

Introduction iv

Question and answer bank

Chapter tasks	**Questions**	**Answers**
1 Business documentation	3	141
2 The books of prime entry	10	144
3 VAT and discounts	19	148
4 Recording credit sales	27	153
5 Recording credit purchases	38	159
6 Double entry bookkeeping (part 1)	52	165
7 Double entry bookkeeping (part 2)	62	171
8 Maintaining the cash book	69	175
9 Double entry for sales and trade receivables	79	181
10 Double entry for purchases and trade payables	104	190
11 Accounting for petty cash	121	198
12 Initial trial balance	134	206
AAT AQ2016 sample assessment	211	229
BPP practice assessment 1	239	257
BPP practice assessment 2	267	289
BPP practice assessment 3	301	323
BPP practice assessment 4	335	357

INTRODUCTION

This is BPP Learning Media's AAT Question Bank for *Bookkeeping Transactions*. It is part of a suite of ground-breaking resources produced by BPP Learning Media for AAT assessments.

This Question Bank has been written in conjunction with the BPP Course Book, and has been carefully designed to enable students to practise all of the learning outcomes and assessment criteria for the units that make up *Bookkeeping Transactions.* It is fully up to date as at April 2016 and reflects both the AAT's qualification specification and the sample assessment provided by the AAT.

This Question Bank contains these key features:

- Tasks corresponding to each chapter of the Course Book. Some tasks are designed for learning purposes, others are of assessment standard

- AAT's AQ2016 sample assessment and answers for *Bookkeeping Transactions* and further BPP practice assessments

The emphasis in all tasks and assessments is on the practical application of the skills acquired.

VAT

You may find tasks throughout this Question Bank that need you to calculate or be aware of a rate of VAT. This is stated at 20% in these examples and questions.

Approaching the assessment

When you sit the assessment it is very important that you follow the on screen instructions. This means you need to carefully read the instructions, both on the introduction screens and during specific tasks.

When you access the assessment you should be presented with an introductory screen with information similar to that shown below (taken from the introductory screen from the AAT's AQ2016 Sample Assessment for *Bookkeeping Transactions*).

We have provided this **sample assessment** to help you familiarise yourself with our e-assessment environment. It is designed to demonstrate as many of the possible question types you may find in a live assessment. It is not designed to be used on its own to determine whether you are ready for a live assessment.

At the end of this sample assessment you will receive an immediate assessment result.

Assessment information:

You have **2 hours** to complete this sample assessment.

This assessment contains **10 tasks** and you should attempt to complete **every** task.
Each task is independent. You will not need to refer to your answers to previous tasks.
Read every task carefully to make sure you understand what is required.

Where the date is relevant, it is given in the task data.

Both minus signs and brackets can be used to indicate negative numbers **unless** task instructions state otherwise.

You must use a full stop to indicate a decimal point. For example, write 100.57 NOT 100,57 or 100 57

You may use a comma to indicate a number in the thousands, but you don't have to. For example, 10000 and 10,000 are both acceptable.

The tasks in this assessment are set in different business situations where the following apply:

- All businesses use a manual bookkeeping system.
- Double entry takes place in the general ledger. Individual accounts of trade receivables and trade payables are kept in the sales and purchases ledgers as subsidiary accounts.
- The cash book and petty cash book should be treated as part of the double entry system unless the task instructions state otherwise.
- The VAT rate is 20%.

The actual instructions will vary depending on the subject you are studying for. It is very important you read the instructions on the introductory screen and apply them in the assessment. You don't want to lose marks when you know the correct answer just because you have not entered it in the right format.

In general, the rules set out in the AAT Sample Assessments for the subject you are studying for will apply in the real assessment, but you should carefully read the information on this screen again in the real assessment, just to make sure. This screen may also confirm the VAT rate used if applicable.

Introduction

A full stop is needed to indicate a decimal point. We would recommend using minus signs to indicate negative numbers and leaving out the comma signs to indicate thousands, as this results in a lower number of key strokes and less margin for error when working under time pressure. Having said that, you can use whatever is easiest for you as long as you operate within the rules set out for your particular assessment.

You have to show competence throughout the assessment and you should therefore complete all of the tasks. Don't leave questions unanswered.

In some assessments, written or complex tasks may be human marked. In this case you are given a blank space or table to enter your answer into. You are told in the assessments which tasks these are (note: there may be none if all answers are marked by the computer).

If these involve calculations, it is a good idea to decide in advance how you are going to lay out your answers to such tasks by practising answering them on a word document, and certainly you should try all such tasks in this Question Bank and in the AAT's environment using the sample assessment.

When asked to fill in tables, or gaps, never leave any blank even if you are unsure of the answer. Fill in your best estimate.

Note that for some assessments where there is a lot of scenario information or tables of data provided (eg tax tables), you may need to access these via 'pop-ups'. Instructions will be provided on how you can bring up the necessary data during the assessment.

Finally, take note of any task specific instructions once you are in the assessment. For example you may be asked to enter a date in a certain format or to enter a number to a certain number of decimal places.

Grading

To achieve the qualification and to be awarded a grade, you must pass all the mandatory unit assessments, all optional unit assessments (where applicable) and the synoptic assessment.

The AAT Level 2 Foundation Certificate in Accounting will be awarded a grade. This grade will be based on performance across the qualification. Unit assessments and synoptic assessments are not individually graded. These assessments are given a mark that is used in calculating the overall grade.

How overall grade is determined

You will be awarded an overall qualification grade (Distinction, Merit, and Pass). If you do not achieve the qualification you will not receive a qualification certificate, and the grade will be shown as unclassified.

The marks of each assessment will be converted into a percentage mark and rounded up or down to the nearest whole number. This percentage mark is then weighted according to the weighting of the unit assessment or synoptic assessment within the qualification. The resulting weighted assessment percentages are combined to arrive at a percentage mark for the whole qualification.

Grade definition	Percentage threshold
Distinction	90–100%
Merit	80–89%
Pass	70–79%
Unclassified	0–69%
	Or failure to pass one or more assessment/s

Re-sits

Some AAT qualifications such as the AAT Foundation Certificate in Accounting have restrictions in place for how many times you are able to re-sit assessments. Please refer to the AAT website for further details.

You should only be entered for an assessment when you are well prepared and you expect to pass the assessment.

AAT qualifications

The material in this book may support the following AAT qualifications:

AAT Foundation Certificate in Accounting Level 2, AAT Foundation Certificate in Accounting at SCQF Level 5 and Certificate: Accounting Technician (Level 3 AATSA).

Supplements

From time to time we may need to publish supplementary materials to one of our titles. This can be for a variety of reasons. From a small change in the AAT unit guidance to new legislation coming into effect between editions.

You should check our supplements page regularly for anything that may affect your learning materials. All supplements are available free of charge on our supplements page on our website at:

www.bpp.com/learning-media/about/students

Improving material and removing errors

There is a constant need to update and enhance our study materials in line with both regulatory changes and new insights into the assessments.

From our team of authors BPP appoints a subject expert to update and improve these materials for each new edition.

Their updated draft is subsequently technically checked by another author and from time to time non-technically checked by a proof reader.

We are very keen to remove as many numerical errors and narrative typos as we can but given the volume of detailed information being changed in a short space of time we know that a few errors will sometimes get though our net.

We apologise in advance for any inconvenience that an error might cause. We continue to look for new ways to improve these study materials and would welcome your suggestions. If you have any comments about this book, please email nisarahmed@bpp.com or write to Nisar Ahmed, AAT Head of Programme, BPP Learning Media Ltd, BPP House, Aldine Place, London W12 8AA.

Question Bank

Bookkeeping Transactions Question Bank

Chapter 1 Business documentation

The tasks in this Question Bank are set in different business situations where the following apply:

- All businesses use a manual bookkeeping system.

- Double entry takes place in the general ledger. Individual accounts of trade receivables and trade payables are kept in the sales and purchases ledgers as subsidiary accounts.

- The cash book and petty cash book should be treated as part of the double entry system unless the task instructions state otherwise.

- The VAT rate is 20%.

Task 1.1

For each of the following transactions state whether they are cash or credit transactions:

	Cash transaction ✓	Credit transaction ✓
Purchase of goods for £200 payable by cash in one week's time		
Writing a cheque for the purchase of a new computer		
Sale of goods to a customer where the invoice accompanies the goods		
Receipt of a cheque from a customer for goods purchased today		
Purchase of goods where payment is due in three weeks' time		

Task 1.2

When a supplier delivers goods to a customer, the customer will expect to receive in due course:

✓	
	A credit note
	A remittance advice
	A petty cash voucher
	An invoice

Task 1.3

A customer wishes to return faulty goods to a credit supplier.

Which document should the customer send with the return?

✓	
	A credit note
	A goods received note
	A goods returned note
	An invoice

Task 1.4

Freddie wishes to purchase some desks from Joe, his credit supplier.

(a) **Which document should Joe issue to Freddie at each stage of this sales process?**

	Document issued by Joe
Freddie asks Joe for a quote on the cost of 14 desks	▼
Joe delivers 14 desks to Freddie	▼
Joe requests payment from Freddie	▼
Freddie pays his invoice and takes a prompt payment discount	▼

Picklist:

Credit note
Customer order
Delivery note
Goods received note
Goods returned note
Invoice
Quotation
Remittance advice

(b) Which document should Freddie create at each stage of the purchase process?

	Document created by Freddie	
Freddie places an order with Joe for 14 desks		▼
Freddie accepts in to his warehouse delivery of 14 desks from Joe		▼
Freddie returns one faulty desk to Joe		▼
Freddie pays his invoice		▼

Picklist:

Credit note
Customer order
Delivery note
Goods received note
Goods returned note
Invoice
Purchase order
Remittance advice
Sales order

Task 1.5

Ken trades in exotic dress materials. He has a large number of small suppliers. He likes to keep all invoices and credit notes from each supplier together in a file for that supplier.

Which sort of coding system would be most appropriate for Ken to use when devising a unique code number for each supplier?

✓	
	An alpha-numeric system
	A numeric system

Task 1.6

JMC Ltd allocates a customer code to each of its customers as shown below. The codes are made up of the first two letters of the customer's name, followed by the number of the ledger page allocated to each customer in that alphabetical group.

Customer name	Customer code
Baxters Ltd	Ba01
Britoil	Br02
Drumbuie Ltd	Dr01
Drumchapel Ltd	Dr02
Joulie Walker	Jo01
Walkers Ltd	Wa01
William Grant Ltd	Wi02
Whyte and Mackay	Wh03

JMC Ltd has two new credit customers which need to be allocated a customer code.

Insert the relevant customer codes for each customer.

Customer	Customer code
Caledonian Ltd	
Jury's Brewery Ltd	

Task 1.7

Complete the sentence

In order to identify how much is owed to a supplier at any point in time, purchases invoices are coded with a:

▼

Picklist:

Customer code
General ledger code
Product code
Supplier code

Task 1.8

Sumberton Ltd codes all purchase invoices with a supplier code **and** a general ledger code. A selection of the codes used is given below.

Supplier	Supplier Code
Casaubon's	PL012
Frankie's Leatherware	PL128
Jane Peel Ltd	PL244
Trinder and Papp	PL301
Wishburton Ltd	PL666

Item	General Ledger Code
Leather bags	GL001
Canvass bags	GL002
Wheeled cases	GL003
Carry cases	GL004
Accessories	GL005

This is an invoice received from a supplier.

Jane Peel Ltd 56 Ward End Road, Doristown DO9 3YU VAT Registration No. 134 1452 22	
Sumberton Ltd Sumberton House 10 Main Road Sawlow SA7 5LD 23 December 20XX	
10 leather bags (product code R245L) @ £17.50 each	£175.00
VAT @ 20%	£35.00
Total	£210.00

(a)   Select which codes would be used to code this invoice.

Supplier code	▼
General ledger code	▼

Picklist:

GL001
GL002
GL003
GL004
GL005
PL012
PL128
PL244
PL301
PL666

(b) Complete the sentence.

In order to identify how much has been spent on a particular product for resale at any point in time, purchases invoices are coded with a

Picklist:

Customer code
General ledger code
Product code
Supplier code

Task 1.9

Ken trades in exotic dress materials. He codes all purchase invoices with a supplier code **and** a general ledger code. A selection of the codes used is given below.

Supplier	Supplier Code
Henderson Co	HEN562
Mack Materials	MAC930
Vinceroy Ltd	VIN234
Streamers	STR220
AVR Partners	AVR001

Product	General Ledger Code
Lace	GL501
Calico	GL502

Product	General Ledger Code
Seersucker	GL503
Cambric	GL504
Velvet	GL505

This is an invoice received from a supplier.

Vinceroy Ltd
17 Fall Road, Agburton AG5 2WE
VAT Registration No. 783 2873 33

Invoice number: 892

Ken's Exotics 1 Bath Street Cembury, CE11 9SD	5 Feb 20XX
20 metres .... Velvet @ £7.00 per metre	£140.00
VAT @ 20%	£ 28.00
Total	£168.00

(a) **Select which codes would be used to code this invoice.**

Supplier account code	▼
General ledger code	▼

Picklist:

AVR001
GL501
GL502
GL503
GL504
GL505
HEN562
MAC930
STR220
VIN234

(b) **Why is it necessary to use a general ledger code?**

▼

Picklist:

To help trace relevant accounts quickly and easily
To make sure the correct balances are calculated
To prevent fraud

Chapter 2 The books of prime entry

Task 2.1

Kendo Ltd trades in exotic dress materials. On 7 August, he is preparing an invoice for goods of £100 plus VAT, for a customer, VXT Ltd.

What will be the amounts entered in the sales day book when the invoice has been prepared?

Sales day book

Date 20XX	Details	Invoice number	Total £	VAT £	Net £
7 August	▼	172			

Picklist:

Kendo Ltd
VXT Ltd

Task 2.2

Kendo has prepared the following invoice.

Kendo Ltd
VAT Registration number 369 4453 00
Invoice No. 365
To: R Hart   15 June 20XX
£
450 product code MM12 @
£1.20 each   540.00
VAT @ 20%   108.00
Total   648.00
Terms: Net monthly account

How will this invoice be entered in to Kendo Ltd's sales day book?

Sales day book

Date 20XX	Details	Invoice number	Total £	VAT £	Net £
15 June	▼				

Picklist:

Kendo Ltd
R Hart

Task 2.3

Natural Productions is a small business that manufactures a variety of soaps and bath products which it sells directly to shops. During January 20XX the following credit sales to customers took place:

Invoice No. 6237 to Hoppers Ltd £547 plus VAT
Invoice No. 6238 to Body Perfect £620 plus VAT
Invoice No. 6239 to Esporta Leisure £346 plus VAT
Invoice No. 6240 to Langans Beauty £228 plus VAT
Invoice No. 6241 to Body Perfect £548 plus VAT
Invoice No. 6242 to Superior Products £221 plus VAT
Invoice No. 6243 to Esporta Leisure £416 plus VAT
Invoice No. 6244 to Hoppers Ltd £238 plus VAT
Invoice No. 6245 to Langans Beauty £274 plus VAT

You are required to:

(a) **Enter these transactions into the sales day book given below.**

(b) **Cast the columns of the sales day book and check that they cross cast.**

Sales day book

Customer		Invoice number	Total £	VAT £	Net £
	▼	6237			
	▼	6238			
	▼	6239			
	▼	6240			
	▼	6241			
	▼	6242			
	▼	6243			
	▼	6244			
	▼	6245			

Picklist:

Body Perfect
Esporta Leisure
Hoppers Ltd
Landans Beauty
Natural Productions
Superior Products

Cross-cast check:

	£
Net	
VAT	
Total	

....

Task 2.4

During January the following credit notes were issued by Natural Productions to various customers:

Credit note No. 1476 to Hoppers Ltd £68.70 plus VAT

Credit note No. 1477 to Esporta Leisure £89.20 plus VAT

Credit note No. 1478 to Superior Products £11.75 plus VAT

Record the credit notes in the appropriate day book by:

- **Selecting the correct daybook title and**
- **Making the necessary entries.**

Day book:	▼

Picklist:

Purchases day book
Purchases returns day book
Sales day book
Sales returns day book

Customer	Credit note number	Total £	VAT £	Net £
▼	1476			
▼	1477			
▼	1478			

Picklist:

Esporta Leisure
Hoppers Ltd
Natural Productions
Superior Products

....

Task 2.5

Natural Productions manufactures a variety of soaps and bath products. It buys materials for the manufacturing process from a number of suppliers on credit. It also buys other items such as stationery on credit. During January 20XX Natural Productions received the following invoices from credit suppliers:

P J Phillips VAT Registration number 436 4472 01		W J Jones VAT Registration number 564 4432 89	
Invoice No. 03576		Invoice No. 18435	
To: Natural Products	4 Jan 20XX	To: Natural Products	6 Jan 20XX
	£		£
225 soap dispensers	357.00	Stationery	210.00
VAT @ 20%	71.40	VAT @ 20%	42.00
Total	428.40	Total	252.00
Terms: Net monthly account		Terms: Net monthly account	

Record the invoices in the appropriate day book by:

- **Selecting the correct day book title and**
- **Making the necessary entries.**

Day book:	▼

Picklist:

Discounts allowed day book
Discounts received day book
Purchases day book
Purchases returns day book
Sales day book
Sales returns day book

Date	Supplier	Invoice number	Total £	VAT £	Purchases (materials) £	Stationery £
		▼				
		▼				

Picklist:

Natural Productions
P J Phillips
W J Jones

Task 2.6

Natural Productions manufactures a variety of soaps and bath products. It buys materials for the manufacturing process from a number of suppliers on credit. It also buys other items such as stationery and packaging on credit. During January 20XX Natural Productions received the following invoices from credit suppliers:

12 Jan Invoice No. 03598 from P J Phillips £413 plus VAT for materials
16 Jan Invoice No. 28423 from Packing Supplies £268 plus VAT for packaging
19 Jan Invoice No. 18478 from Trenter Ltd £521 plus VAT for materials
20 Jan Invoice No. 84335 from O & P Ltd £624 plus VAT for materials
24 Jan Invoice No. 28444 from Packing Supplies £164 plus VAT for packaging
28 Jan Invoice No. 18491 from Trenter Ltd £368 plus VAT for materials
31 Jan Invoice No. 43681 from W J Jones £104 plus VAT for stationery

Record the invoices in the appropriate day book by:

- **Selecting the correct day book title and**
- **Making the necessary entries.**

Day book:	▼

Picklist:

Discounts allowed day book
Discounts received day book
Purchases day book
Purchases returns day book
Sales day book
Sales returns day book

Date	Supplier	Invoice number	Total £	VAT £	Purchases (materials) £	Stationery £	Packaging £
12 Jan	▼	03598					
16 Jan	▼	28423					
19 Jan	▼	18478					
20 Jan	▼	84335					
24 Jan	▼	28444					
28 Jan	▼	18491					
31 Jan	▼	43681					

Picklist:

Natural Productions
O & P Ltd
Packing Supplies
P J Phillips
Trenter Ltd
W J Jones

Task 2.7

During January Natural Productions received the following credit notes from suppliers.

P J Phillips VAT Registration number 436 4472 01		W J Jones VAT Registration number 564 4432 89	
Credit note No. 04216		Credit note No. CN 0643	
To: Natural Products	10 Jan 20XX	To: Natural Products	16 Jan 20XX
	£		£
Materials	98.00	Stationery	56.00
VAT @ 20%	19.60	VAT @ 20%	11.20
Total	117.60	Total	67.20
Terms: Net monthly account		Terms: Net monthly account	

Record the credit notes in the appropriate day book by:

- **Selecting the correct day book title and**
- **Making the necessary entries.**

Day book:	

Picklist:

Discounts allowed day book
Discounts received day book
Purchases day book
Purchases returns day book
Sales day book
Sales returns day book

Date	Supplier	Credit note number	Total £	VAT £	Purchases (materials) £	Stationery £	Packaging £
10 Jan	▼	▼					
16 Jan	▼	▼					

Picklist:

Natural Productions
P J Phillips
W J Jones
04216
CN 0643

Task 2.8

You work in the accounts department of Southfield Electrical. You have been given the two credit notes below.

Southfield Electrical	
VAT Registration number 569 5242 89	
Credit note No. 08650	
Customer No. SL 44 21 Sept 20XX	
To: Whitehill Superstores	
	£
Zanpoint fridge	330.00
Less 10% trade discount	33.00
	297.00
VAT @ 20%	59.40
Total	356.40
Reason: damaged goods	

Southfield Electrical	
VAT Registration number 569 5242 89	
Credit note No. 08651	
Customer No. SL 15 23 Sept 20XX	
To: Dagwell Enterprises	
	£
6 Temax coffee maker @ 40.00 each	240.00
Less 15% trade discount	36.00
	204.00
VAT @ 20%	40.80
Total	244.80
Reason: goods not ordered	

Complete the sales returns day book by:

- **Entering the credit notes.**
- **Totalling the columns.**

Sales returns day book

Date	Customer		Credit note number	Customer code		Gross total £	VAT £	Net £
21 Sep		▼			▼			
23 Sep		▼			▼			
	Totals							

Picklist:

Dagwell Enterprises
Southfield Electrical
Whitehill Superstores
SL 15
SL 44

....

Task 2.9

Given below are the only four purchase invoices received by Short Furniture in the week ending 27 January 20XX. You are also given an extract from the supplier codes listing.

27 Jan Invoice No. 09642 from Ephraim Supplies £291.00 plus VAT for wood
27 Jan Invoice No. 06932 from Cavendish Woods £705.10 plus VAT for wood
27 Jan Invoice No. 67671 from Calverley Bros £145.60 plus VAT for polish
27 Jan Invoice No. 36004 from Culverden & Co £57.40 plus VAT for other purchases

Supplier codes listing

Calverley Bros	PL03
Cavendish Woods	PL14
Culverden & Co	PL23
Ephraim Supplies	PL39

Complete the purchases day book by:

- **Entering the invoices – note that purchases are analysed into wood, polish and other.**

- **Totalling the columns.**

Purchases day book

Date	Supplier	Invoice number	Supplier code	Total £	VAT £	Net £	Wood Purchases £	Polish purchases £	Other purchases £
	▼		▼						
	▼		▼						
	▼		▼						
	▼		▼						

Picklist:

Calverley Bros
Cavendish Woods
Culverden & Co
Ephraim Supplies
PL03
PL14
PL23
PL39

Task 2.10

You work for Smith & Co. Credit notes to customers have been prepared and partially entered in the sales returns day book, as shown below.

(a) **Complete the entries in the sales returns day book by inserting the appropriate figures for each credit note.**

(b) **Total the last five columns of the sales returns day book.**

Sales returns day book

Date 20XX	Details	Credit note number	Total £	VAT £	Net £	Bags returns £	Suitcases returns £
30 Nov	Shrier Goods	562		104		520	
30 Nov	Gringles Co	563	408				340
30 Nov	Lester plc	564	1,068		890	890	
	Totals						

Chapter 3 VAT and discounts

Task 3.1

Ken trades in exotic dress materials. He has many credit customers who operate in the same trade as him and he routinely offers these customers a discount off the list price of his goods in order to maintain good relations.

What type of discount is this an example of?

✓	
	A trade discount
	A prompt payment discount
	A bulk discount

Task 3.2

VAT is a tax on consumer expenditure which a VAT registered business must collect from its customers.

Who is VAT paid over to?

✓	
	The Home Office
	The Treasury
	The Inland Revenue
	HM Revenue & Customs

Task 3.3

On your desk is a pile of sales invoices that have already had the price of the goods entered onto them and been totalled. The customers are to be given a 15% trade discount.

Calculate the trade discount and net total to be included on each invoice.

Goods total	Trade discount £	Net total £
£416.80		
£105.60		
£96.40		
£263.20		
£351.00		

Task 3.4

On your desk there is a pile of invoices which have the net total entered.

Calculate the VAT charge and the invoice total to be included on each invoice.

Net total	VAT £	Gross total £
£258.90		
£316.80		
£82.60		
£152.70		
£451.30		

Task 3.5

The following gross totals include VAT.

Calculate the amount of VAT on each invoice and the net amount of the invoice.

Gross total £	VAT £	Net total £
145.20		
66.90		
246.60		
35.40		
125.40		

Task 3.6

The following purchases have been made for cash inclusive of VAT.

Calculate the amount of VAT on each purchase and the net amount of the purchase.

Gross total £	VAT £	Net total £
252.66		
169.20		
48.60		
104.28		
60.48		
822.60		

Task 3.7

These customers have all been offered a prompt payment discount of 3% if they pay within 10 days.

Calculate the amount each customer would pay if they pay within 10 days and take the prompt payment discount.

Customer	Gross invoice total £	Amount £
J Smith	258	
Anchorage Ltd	312	
VIP Ltd	84	
Blue House Ltd	150	

Task 3.8

A sales invoice is being prepared for goods supplied, as shown in the customer order below. A bulk discount of 2% is given for all orders where more than 100 products have been ordered.

Customer order

Jules Ltd
Order number 8965
Please supply: 2 May 20XX
200 microwaves
@ £35.00 each less 5% trade discount.

Calculate the amounts to be included in the invoice.

	£
Net amount before discounts	
Net amount after discounts	
VAT	
Total	

Task 3.9

An invoice for £1,280 plus VAT has been sent to JKF Ltd offering a prompt payment discount of 10% for payment within 14 days.

(a) What is the amount JKF Ltd will pay if they pay within 14 days?

£	

JKF Ltd pays the invoice within 14 days and takes the prompt payment discount.

(b) Complete the table below to show the amounts to be included on the credit note for JKF Ltd.

Credit note

Amount	£
Net amount	
VAT	
Gross amount	

Task 3.10

The credit note below has been sent to a customer in respect of a prompt payment discount.

Anchor Supplies Ltd
Horwich Way
Bolton BL8 3XU

VAT Registration No. 424 5242 42

PROMPT PAYMENT DISCOUNT CREDIT NOTE

Shipper Ltd   Customer account code: SHIP001
24 George Street
Rochdale   Invoice no: 298
RC3 4HJ

Credit note no: 223   Date: 15 October 20XX

Net £	VAT £	Gross £
56.00	11.20	67.20

Record the credit note in the appropriate day book by:

- **Selecting the correct daybook title and**
- **Making the necessary entries.**

Day book:	▼

Picklist:

Discounts allowed day book
Discounts received day book
Purchases day book
Purchases returns day book
Sales day book
Sales returns day book

Date 20XX	Details	Credit note number	Total £	VAT £	Net £
15 Oct	▼	223			

Picklist:

Anchor Supplies Ltd
Shipper Ltd

Task 3.11

The credit note below has been received from a supplier in respect of a prompt payment discount.

Rent a Van Ltd
31 Cannon Way, Manchester
MZ2 8BS

VAT Registration No. 569 5242 89

PROMPT PAYMENT DISCOUNT CREDIT NOTE

Pop Ice Cream ltd   Customer account code: POP003
4 Goodge Street
Ainsworth   Invoice no: 569
Lancs AL52 2FC

Credit note no: 11   Date: 10 November 20XX

Net £	VAT £	Gross £
103.00	20.60	123.60

Required

Record the credit note in the appropriate day book by:

- **Selecting the correct day book title and**
- **Making the necessary entries.**

Day book:	▼

Picklist:

Discounts allowed day book
Discounts received day book
Purchases day book
Purchases returns day book
Sales day book
Sales returns day book

Date 20XX	Details		Credit note number	Total £	VAT £	Net £
10 Nov		▼	11			

Picklist:

Pop Ice Cream Ltd
Rent a Van Ltd

Task 3.12

An invoice is being prepared by Sumberton Ltd to be sent to Meering Ltd for £2,000 plus VAT. A prompt payment discount of 4% will be offered for payment within 10 days.

(a) **What is the amount Sumberton Ltd should receive if payment is made within 10 days?**

£ _____

(b) **What is the amount Sumberton Ltd should receive if payment is not made within 10 days?**

£ _____

Task 3.13

Sumberton Ltd offers some established customers a discount of 4% whatever the size of their order and irrespective of when they pay.

What is the name of this type of discount?

_____ ▼

Picklist:

Bulk discount
Prompt payment discount
Trade discount

Task 3.14

Show whether the following statements are true or false.

	True ✓	False ✓
The book of prime entry for discounts allowed is the petty cash book		
Input tax is the VAT suffered on purchases		
A goods received note is a primary document for recording in the accounting records		

Chapter 4 Recording credit sales

Task 4.1

Ken trades in exotic dress materials. A new customer has phoned up with an enquiry about buying some materials from Ken.

What should Ken send the customer?

✓	
	A delivery note
	A price list
	A goods received note
	A statement of account

Task 4.2

Ken wishes to analyse his sales so that he can distinguish between those made to UK customers and those from abroad.

What is the best way for him to do this?

✓	
	Analyse every invoice into a separate column of his analysed sales day book
	Allocate one of two sales codes to each invoice and use this to write up the invoices in the analysed sales day book
	Allocate invoice numbers on a randomised basis
	Use a different sequence of invoice numbers for each customer

Task 4.3

On 8 January 20XX, Southfield Electrical received the following purchase order from Whitehill Superstores. The goods were delivered the following day.

Southfield Electrical's customer files show the following information.

Customer name	Customer code	Trade discount	Prompt payment discount
Whitehill Superstores	SL 44	10%	4% – 10 days

Whitehill Superstores
28 Whitehill Park
Benham DR6 5LM

Purchase Order 32431

Southfield Electrical   4 Jan 20XX
Industrial Estate
Benham DR6 2FF

Please supply 8 units of product code 6260 Hosch
Tumble Dryer
@ £300.00 each, plus VAT.

Complete the ten boxes in the sales invoice below.

Southfield Electrical
Industrial Estate
Benham DR6 2FF
VAT registration no: 569 5242 89

SALES INVOICE 57104

Date: [▼]

To: Whitehill Superstores   Customer account code: [   ]
       28 Whitehill Park

       Benham, DR6 5LM   Purchase order no: [   ]

Quantity of units	Product code	Price each £	Total amount after trade discount £	VAT £	Total £

Terms: [▼]

Picklist:

4 Jan 20XX
8 Jan 20XX
9 Jan 20XX
Net monthly account
30 days net
4% prompt payment discount for payment within 10 days
10% trade discount

Task 4.4

On 18 May 20XX, Southfield Electrical received the following purchase order from Harper & Sons Ltd. The goods were delivered the following day.

Southfield Electrical's customer files show the following discount policy.

Customer name	Customer code	Trade discount	Prompt payment discount
Harper & Sons	SL 26	5%	3% – 14 days

Harper & Sons also receives a bulk discount of 5% if the net amount of their order, after deducting trade discount, is over £1,000.

Harper & Sons
30 High Street
Benham DR6 4ST

Purchase Order 04367

Southfield Electrical   16 May 20XX
Industrial Estate
Benham DR6 2FF

Please supply 6 units of product code 6370 Hosch
Washing Machine
@ £260.00 each, plus VAT.

Complete the ten boxes in the sales invoice on the following page.

Southfield Electrical
Industrial Estate
Benham DR6 2FF
VAT registration no: 569 5242 89

SALES INVOICE 57105

Date: [▼]

To: Harper & Sons   Customer account code: [   ]
      30 High Street

      Benham, DR6 4ST   Purchase order no: [   ]

Quantity of units	Product code	Price each £	Total amount after discounts £	VAT £	Total £

Terms: [▼]

Picklist:

16 May 20XX
18 May 20XX
19 May 20XX
Net monthly account
30 days net
3% prompt payment discount for payment within 14 days
5% bulk discount
5% trade discount

Task 4.5

On 20 Oct Whitehill Superstores received an invoice from Southfield Electrical. The invoice is shown below together with the delivery note and the purchase order.

Invoice

Southfield Electrical
Industrial Estate, Benham DR6 2FF
VAT Registration No. 569 5242 89

To: Whitehill Superstores   19 Oct 20XX

Invoice No. 56501

Delivery note 34816
Purchase order 385

	£
15 product 9046 @ £15 each	225.00
VAT @ 20%	45.00
Total	270.00

Terms

Terms: Net monthly account

Delivery note

Southfield Electrical
Industrial Estate, Benham DR6 2FF
VAT Registration No. 569 5242 89

Delivery note 34816

18 Oct 20XX

To:

Whitehill Superstore
28 Whitehill Park
Benham DR6 5LM

Please receive 12 product 9406
Kensharp Toaster.

Purchase order

Whitehill Superstores
Order number 32202

Please supply: 16 Oct 20XX

15 Kensharp Toaster product code 9406

@ £15.00 each less 5% trade discount

As agreed, terms of payment are 3% discount for payment by the end of the month.

(a) Check the delivery note, the invoice and the purchase order and answer the following questions.

Questions	Yes ✓	No ✓
Has the correct amount of goods been delivered?		
Has the correct product been delivered?		
Have the correct codes been used on the invoice?		
Has the correct discount been applied?		

(b) **Based on the amounts actually delivered to the customer, what should be the correct amounts of the invoice?**

Net amount £	VAT amount £	Gross amount £

Task 4.6

Given below is a credit note and a goods returned note from a customer, Whitehill Superstores. Whitehill Superstores receives 20% trade discount on all orders.

Credit note

Southfield Electrical
Industrial Estate, Benham DR6 2FF
VAT Registration No. 569 5242 89

To: Whitehill Superstores   22 Oct 20XX

Credit note No. 08669

Purchase order 40102

	£
3 product 4770 @ £220 each	660.00
VAT @ 20%	132.00
Total	792.00

Reason: ordered in error

Goods returned note

Whitehill Superstores
28 Whitehill Park
Benham DR6 5LM

To: Southfield Electrical   19 Oct 20XX

Goods returned note No. 56

Purchase order 40102

4 product 4770 @ £220 each

Reason: faulty goods

Identify any discrepancies on the credit note by drawing a line between each left hand box and then the appropriate right hand box.

| Reason for return |

| VAT calculation |

| Trade discount |

| Quantity |

| Not shown on credit note |

| Incorrectly shown on credit note |

| Correctly shown on credit note |

Task 4.7

Southfield Electrical received a cheque for £516.10 from a credit customer, Hayworth Ltd, on 20 November 20XX. There was no document included with the cheque to show what transactions were included in the payment.

(a) **Show what document the customer should have included with the cheque by circling one document name.**

Document names
Delivery note   Petty cash voucher   Purchase order   Remittance advice note

After contacting Hayworth Ltd, you identify that the payment covers the invoice shown below.

Invoice number	**30227**	
Date:	7 November 20XX	
To:	Hayworth Ltd	
		£
Goods value		448.00
VAT		89.60
Invoice total		537.60

4% prompt payment discount for payment received within 10 days of invoice date, otherwise 30 days net

(b) **Using the picklist below, complete the following statement.**

The cheque from Hayworth Ltd for £516.10 has resulted in an
☐ ▼

This is because Hayworth has taken the ☐ ▼ offered.

This should not have been taken as the cheque arrived ☐ ▼ after the invoice date.

In order to resolve the problem Southfield Electrical should ☐ ▼ from Hayworth Ltd for £ ☐ which will clear the outstanding balance.

Picklist:

13 days
14 days
less than 10 days
overpayment
prompt payment discount
request a credit note
request an invoice
request another cheque
trade discount
underpayment

Task 4.8

Southfield Electrical received a cheque for £709.48 from a credit customer, Harper & Sons, with a remittance advice stating the payment was for invoice **30256**, shown below. The cheque was received on 19 November 20XX.

Invoice number	**30256**	
Date:	12 November XX	
To:	Harper & Sons	
		£
Goods value		620.00
VAT		124.00
Invoice total		744.00

4% prompt payment discount for payment received within 10 days of invoice date, otherwise 30 days net

Using the picklist below, complete the following statement.

The cheque from Harper & Sons for £709.48 has resulted in an [▾]

Harper & Sons paid within the time limit for the [▾] offered by Southfield Electrical.

However, they [▾] the discount.

In order to resolve the problem Southfield Electrical should [▾] from Harper & Sons for £ [ ] which will clear the outstanding balance.

Picklist:

correctly calculated
incorrectly calculated
overpayment
prompt payment discount
request a credit note
request an invoice
request another cheque
trade discount
underpayment

Task 4.9

On 21 December Sumberton Ltd delivered the following goods to a credit customer, Gringles Co.

Sumberton Ltd
Sumberton House
10 Main Road
Sawlow
SA7 5LD

Delivery note No. 6734527
21 December 20XX

Gringles Co   Customer account code: SL637
Unit 18 Radley Estate
Sawlow
SA7 7VB

80 leather shoulder bags, product code L736B.

The list price of the goods was £100 per box of five bags plus VAT. Gringles Co is to be given a 15% bulk discount and a 4% discount if the invoice is paid within 10 days.

Complete the invoice below.

Sumberton Ltd
Sumberton House,
10 Main Road
Sawlow
SA7 5LD

VAT Registration No. 536 3723 77

Gringles Co   Customer account code: SL637
Unit 18 Radley Estate
Sawlow
SA7 7VB

Date: 22 December 20XX

Invoice No: 12901
Delivery note number: 6734527

Quantity of goods	Product code	Total list price £	Net amount after bulk discount £	VAT £	Gross £

Task 4.10

The account shown below is in the sales ledger of Sumberton Ltd. A remittance advice for an automated payment of £2,807 has now been received from this customer.

Meering Ltd

Date 20XX	Details	Amount £	Date 20XX	Details	Amount £
6 October	Sales invoice 12624	1,756	10 October	Sales returns credit note 501	78
11 November	Sales invoice 12711	2,918	17 November	Sales returns credit note 555	111
7 December	Sales invoice 12813	2,384	30 November	Bank	1,678

Which outstanding item has not been included in the payment of £2,807?

▼

Picklist:

Bank
Sales invoice 12624
Sales invoice 12711
Sales invoice 12813
Sales returns credit note 501
Sales returns credit note 555

Task 4.11

The following is a summary of transactions with Diamond Bags, a new credit customer.

£1,902 re invoice 12905 of 10 December
£219 re credit note 701 of 12 December
£733 re invoice 12916 of 30 December
Cheque for £1,668 received 31 December
Prompt payment discount £15 taken 31 December

Complete the statement of account below. Enter all amounts as a positive value.

Sumberton Ltd
Sumberton House
10 Main Road
Sawlow
SA7 5LD

To: Diamond Bags		Date: 31 December 20XX	
Date 20XX	**Details**	**Transaction amount £**	**Outstanding amount £**
10 December	Invoice 12905		
12 December	Credit note 701		
30 December	Invoice 12916		
31 December	Cheque		
31 December	Discount taken		

Task 4.12

Ken trades in exotic dress materials. The following is a summary of his transactions with Crowley Ltd, a new credit customer.

£627 re invoice 1540 of 15 September
£728 re invoice 1560 of 29 September
£46 re credit note 89 of 3 October
£1,209 re invoice 1580 of 10 October
Cheque for £581 received 15 October

Complete the statement of account below by:

- **Dragging and dropping the appropriate details and transaction amount below into the second column.**

- **Entering the outstanding amount after every transaction into the final column.**

STATEMENT OF ACCOUNT
Ken's Exotics
1 Bath Street
Cembury, CE11 9SD

To: Crowley Ltd		Date: 31 October 20XX
Date 20XX	**Details and transaction amount £**	**Outstanding amount £**
15 Sept		
29 Sept		
3 Oct		
10 Oct		
15 Oct		

Details and transaction amount (£):

Cheque - £581	Credit note 89 - £46	Invoice 1540 - £627
Invoice 1560 - £728	Invoice 1580 - £1,209	

Chapter 5 Recording credit purchases

Task 5.1

Ken trades in exotic dress materials.

Complete the following statement:

When a supplier delivers materials to him he retains the supplier's delivery note and also prepares [▼] once he has had a chance to inspect the quality of the items.

Picklist:

An invoice
A goods received note
A remittance advice

Task 5.2

Complete the following statement:

A code which will help Ken to classify the different types of material purchase when completing his analysed purchases day book is

	✓
A supplier code	
A product code	

Task 5.3

Ken has been offered a prompt payment discount by one of his suppliers of '2% for payment within 10 days'. He receives an invoice dated 10 June on 12 June with a total of £239.20, excluding VAT. He wishes to take advantage of the discount.

(a) By what date must the supplier receive the payment?

[▼]

Picklist:

19 June
20 June
21 June
22 June

(b) How much should Ken pay the supplier on that date?

£ [   ]

···

Task 5.4

You work for Newmans, a music shop, in the accounts department and one of your responsibilities is to organise the payments to suppliers. You have been off sick for the last week and a half and therefore it is urgent that you consider the invoices that are on your desk requiring payment.

Newmans' policy is to pay any invoices that are due each Friday. When a cheque is written on a Friday it does not then reach the supplier until Monday, ie three days later. If a prompt payment discount is offered by a supplier then this is taken if the discount will still be valid on the Monday. Otherwise the policy is to take the maximum amount of credit available.

Today's date is Friday 27 January 20XX. Thereafter, the following payment dates are 3 February, 10 February and 17 February. Remember that, as payments take three days to reach the supplier, any invoice dated earlier than 7 January with a 30-day period must be paid today, because if they are delayed until 3 February then the payments will not be received until 6 February, more than 30 days after they are due.

The invoices that are on your desk are scheduled below:

Invoice date	Supplier name	Terms	Total £	VAT £	Net £
5 Jan	Henson Press	30 days	336.00	56.00	280.00
8 Jan	GH Publications	30 days	136.80	22.80	114.00
12 Jan	Ely Instruments	20 days 2% discount otherwise 30 days	765.00	127.50	637.50
15 Jan	Hams Instruments	14 days 2.5% discount otherwise 30 days	372.00	62.00	310.00
19 Jan	CD Supplies	10 days 3% discount otherwise 30 days	138.72	23.12	115.60
22 Jan	Jester Press	10 days 3.5% discount otherwise 30 days	156.00	26.00	130.00
22 Jan	Henson Press	30 days	306.00	51.00	255.00

In the schedule given below show the date that each invoice should be paid and the amount for which the cheque should be written out.

Invoice date	Supplier name	Payment date	Amount of cheque £
5 Jan	Henson Press	▼	
8 Jan	GH Publications	▼	
12 Jan	Ely Instruments	▼	
15 Jan	Hams Instruments	▼	
19 Jan	CD Supplies	▼	
22 Jan	Jester Press	▼	
22 Jan	Henson Press	▼	

Picklist:

27 Jan
3 Feb
10 Feb
17 Feb

Task 5.5

Given below is a statement received by your organisation, Edgehill Designs, from one of its credit suppliers, P T Supplies, as at 31 January 20XX. You are instructed to pay all of the invoices less credit notes up to 10 January. Today's date is 7 February.

	PT Supplies 149 Field Road, Darton, DF12 8GH		
	STATEMENT OF ACCOUNT		
To: Edgehill Designs		31 January 20XX	
Date 20XX	Invoice/credit note number	Details	Amount £
6 Jan	Inv 20671	Goods	107
8 Jan	Inv 20692	Goods	157
10 Jan	CN 04722	Goods returned	28
27 Jan	Inv 20718	Goods	120
30 Jan	CN 04786	Goods returned	16

(a) Complete the remittance advice below by:

- Selecting the date from the picklist in the first column

- Dragging and dropping the appropriate details and transaction amount below into the second column

You only need to enter the relevant invoices and credit notes. Leave blank any rows that are not needed.

Remittance advice	
To: PT Supplies Designs	From: Edgehill
Date: 7 February 20XX	

Date 20XX	Details and transaction amount £
▼	
▼	
▼	
▼	
▼	

Picklist:

6 Jan
8 Jan
10 Jan
27 Jan
30 Jan
7 Feb

Details and transaction amount (£):

Inv 20671 - £107	Inv 20692 - £157	CN 04722 - £28
Inv 20718 - £120	CN 04786 - £16	

(b) **What is the total payment amount to accompany this remittance advice note?**

£

Task 5.6

On 12 July Whitehill Superstores ordered goods from Southfield Electrical who agreed a 10% trade discount and payment terms of 30 days net. The goods were delivered on 15 July and the invoice and goods received note are shown below.

Invoice

Southfield Electrical
Industrial Estate Benham DR6 2FF
VAT Registration No. 569 5242 89

To: Whitehill Superstores Invoice No. 56389	15 Jun 20XX

	£
10 product code 9116 @ £24 each	240.00
VAT @ 20%	48.00
Total	288.00

Terms: Cash on delivery

Goods received note

Whitehill Superstores

Goods received note GRN47422

15 July 20XX

Received from: Southfield Electrical

10 product code 9116 in good condition

(a) **Refer to the information above and the goods received note and identify any discrepancies on the invoice by drawing a line between each left hand box and then the appropriate right hand box.**

| Terms of payment |
| Customer name |
| VAT rate |
| Trade discount |
| Quantity of goods delivered |
| Date |

| Not shown on invoice |
| Incorrectly shown on invoice |
| Correctly shown on invoice |

(b)   What will be the correct amounts on the invoice?

Net amount £	VAT amount £	Gross amount £

Task 5.7

Given below is an invoice received by Dartmouth Supplies and the related purchase order.

Invoice

Dan Industries
Park Rise
Fenbridge DR2 7AD
VAT Registration No. 0621 3384 20

To: Dartmouth Supplies   7 Oct 20XX

Invoice No. 77412

Delivery note 34816
Purchase order 317428

	£
16 product D5345 Rocking chair @ £96.00 each	1,536.00
Less trade discount @ 5%	76.80
	1,459.20
VAT @ 20%	291.84
Total	1,600.04

Terms: 30 days net

Purchase order

Dan Industries
Order number 317428

20 Sept 20XX

Please supply 16 product D4632 Rocking chair @ £96.00 each plus VAT

Discount: 10% trade discount, as agreed

(a) **Check the invoice and the purchase order and answer the following questions.**

	Yes ✓	No ✓
Has the correct purchase price of the rocking chairs been charged?		
Has the correct discount been applied?		
Has the invoice been correctly cast?		
Has the correct product code been used on the invoice?		
Has VAT been charged at the correct rate?		

(b) **What will be the correct amounts on the invoice?**

Net amount £	VAT amount £	Gross amount £

Task 5.8

You work for Bailie Ltd. Shown below is a statement of account received from a credit supplier, Dazzle Ltd, and the supplier's account as shown in the purchases ledger of Bailie Ltd.

Dazzle Ltd
21 Albert Street
Keeley
KE4 7AB

To: Bailie Ltd
5 Purley Road
Keeley
KE5 7LW

STATEMENT OF ACCOUNT

Date 20XX	Reference	Details	Debit £	Credit £	Balance £
1 July	8371	Goods	335		335
3 July	8412	Goods	420		755
7 July	8515	Goods	723		1,478
10 July	CN 3215	Goods returned		250	1,228
16 July		Cheque		485	743

Purchàses ledger – Dazzle Ltd

Date 20XX	Details	Amount £	Date 20XX	Details	Amount £
15 July	Bank – cheque	485	1 July	PDB 8371	335
15 July	Discount received	20	3 July	PDB 8412	420
			7 July	PDB 8515	723

(a) Which item is missing from the statement of account from Dazzle Ltd?

▼

Picklist:

Bank – cheque £485
Credit note 3215 £250
Discount received £20
Invoice 8371 £335
Invoice 8412 £420
Invoice 8515 £723

(b) Which item is missing from the supplier account in Bailie Ltd's purchases ledger?

▼

Picklist:

Cheque £485
Credit note 3215 £250
Discount received £20
Invoice 8371 £335
Invoice 8412 £420
Invoice 8515 £723

(c) Assuming any differences between the statement of account from Dazzle Ltd and the supplier account in Bailie Ltd's purchases ledger are simply due to omission errors, what is the amount owing to Dazzle Ltd?

£ [ ]

....

Task 5.9

A supply of nails has been delivered to Acute Carpentry by Carbon Irons. The purchase order sent from Acute Carpentry, and the invoice from Carbon Irons, are shown below.

Acute Carpentry
Purchase Order No. 78639

To: Carbon Irons

Date: 16 June

Please supply 30 boxes 6 inch nails product code N1106
Purchase price: £20 per box, plus VAT
Discount: less 10% trade discount, as agreed.

Carbon Irons
Invoice No. 2318

Acute Carpentry

18 June

30 .... boxes product code N1106 @ £25 each	£750.00
VAT @ 20%	£150.00
Total	£900.00

Terms: 30 days net

Check the invoice against the purchase order and answer the following questions.

	Yes ✓	No ✓
Has the correct purchase price of the cardboard boxes been charged?		
Has the correct discount been applied?		
What would be the VAT amount charged if the invoice was correct?	£	
What would be the total amount charged if the invoice was correct?	£	

Task 5.10

Ken runs a business trading in exotic dress materials. He sends out cheques to suppliers on the last day of the month following the month of invoice. Below is an extract from Ken's purchases ledger for his supplier, Mack Materials.

Mack Materials

Date 20XX	Details	Amount £	Date 20XX	Details	Amount £
31 May	Bank	890	1 May	Balance b/d	890
19 May	Purchases returns Credit note 43	31	7 May	Purchases Invoice 901	760
			3 June	Purchases Invoice 963	189

(a) **Complete the remittance advice note below. Leave any spare lines blank. Enter all amounts as positive values.**

Ken's Exotics
1 Bath Street

Cembury, CE11 9SD

REMITTANCE ADVICE

To: Mack Materials   Date: 30 June 20XX

Please find attached our cheque in payment of the following amounts.

Invoice number		Credit note number		Amount £
	▼		▼	
	▼		▼	
	▼		▼	
	▼		▼	
Total amount paid				

Picklist:

Balance b/d
Bank
Credit note 43
Invoice 901
Invoice 903

(b) Which of the following statements is true?

	✓
The remittance advice note will be sent to the accounts department at Mack Materials to request that a cheque is raised	
The remittance advice note will be sent to Mack Materials' bank to advise them of the amount being paid	
The remittance advice note will be sent to the customer to advise them of the amount being paid	
The remittance advice note will be sent to the supplier to advise them of the amount being paid	

Task 5.11

Ken has received a statement from a supplier which shows that, as at the end of June 20XX, he owes the supplier £2,876. The purchases ledger account for this supplier shows that at that date Ken only owed £1,290.

Which of the following items would explain the difference?

	✓
Ken has requested a credit note from the supplier for £1,586 which he has not yet received	
Ken sent a cheque for £1,586 to the supplier on 30 June 20XX	
Ken ordered some items from the supplier on 30 June for £1,586 but the goods have not yet been delivered and an invoice has not yet been raised	

Task 5.12

A supply of suitcases has been delivered to Sumberton Ltd by Casaubon's. The purchase order sent from Sumberton Ltd, and the invoice from Casaubon's, are shown below.

Sumberton Ltd **Sumberton House, 10 Main Road** **Sawlow** **SA7 5LD** **Purchase Order No. 7683247**
To: Casaubon's Date: 17 December 20XX Please supply 15 small wheeled cabin cases, product code WCC625 Purchase price: £23 each, plus VAT Discount: less 15% trade discount, as agreed.

Casaubon's
80 Eliot Street, Sawlow SA9 4AC
VAT Registration No. 983 3933 83

Invoice No. 782736

Sumberton Ltd
Sumberton House, 10 Main Road
Sawlow
SA7 5LD

22 December 20XX

15 small wheeled cabin cases product code WCC625 @ £25 each	£375.00
Less trade discount at 5%	£18.75
Net amount	£356.25
VAT @ 20%	£71.25
Total	£427.50

Terms: 30 days net

Check the invoice against the purchase order and answer the following questions.

	Yes ✓	No ✓
Has the correct purchase price of the cabin cases been charged?		
Has the correct discount been applied?		
What would be the VAT amount charged if the invoice was correct?	£	
What would be the total amount charged if the invoice was correct?	£	

···

Task 5.13

Shown below is a statement of account received from a credit supplier, and the supplier's account as shown in the purchases ledger of Sumberton Ltd.

Trinder and Papp
54 Vallais Road
Gosfirth
GO9 5VV

To: Sumberton Ltd
Sumberton House
10 Main Road
Sawlow
SA7 5LD

STATEMENT OF ACCOUNT

Date 20XX	Number	Details	Amount £	Balance £
20 October	10923	Invoice	2,109	2,109
4 November		Payment	−2,099	10
8 November	11004	Invoice	3,188	3,198
10 November	C536	Credit note	−156	3,042
26 November	11342	Invoice	2,185	5,227
28 November	11378	Invoice	1,244	6,471
30 November	C579	Credit note	−320	6,151

Trinder and Papp

Date 20XX	Details	Amount £	Date 20XX	Details	Amount £
4 Nov	Bank – BACS	2,099	20 Oct	Purchases	2,109
4 Nov	Discount	10	8 Nov	Purchases	3,188
10 Nov	Purchases returns	156	26 Nov	Purchases	2,185
			28 Nov	Purchases	1,244

BPP
LEARNING MEDIA

(a) **Which item is missing from the statement of account from Trinder and Papp?**

	▼

Picklist:

Credit note C536
Credit note C579
Discount of £10
Invoice 10923
Invoice 11004
Invoice 11342
Invoice 11378
Payment for £2,099

(b) **Which item is missing from the supplier account in Sumberton Ltd's purchases ledger?**

	▼

Picklist:

Credit note C536
Credit note C579
Discount of £10
Invoice 10923
Invoice 11004
Invoice 11342
Invoice 11378
Payment for £2,099

(c) **Assuming any differences between the statement of account from Trinder and Papp and the supplier account in Sumberton Ltd's purchases ledger are simply due to omission errors, what is the amount owing to Trinder and Papp?**

£ [   ]

(d) **Which of the following statements is true?**

	✓
A credit note adds to the amount owed to the supplier	
A remittance advice note adds to the amount owed to the supplier	
A goods received note adds to the amount owed to the supplier	
An invoice adds to the amount owed to the supplier	

Chapter 6 Double entry bookkeeping (part 1)

Task 6.1

Identify whether each of the following is an asset or a liability:

	Asset ✓	Liability ✓
A trade receivable		
A car used in the business		
A loan from the bank		
A bank overdraft		
Cash in hand		
VAT owed to HMRC		
A trade payable		
Inventory of raw materials		

Task 6.2

Complete the following statements using the word 'debit' or 'credit' in each case:

An increase in an expense is a [ ]

A decrease in a liability is a [ ]

An increase in income is a [ ]

An increase in an asset is a [ ]

An increase in capital is a [ ]

A decrease in an asset is a [ ]

An increase in a liability is a [ ]

A decrease in capital is a [ ]

Task 6.3

(a) **Insert the two effects of each of these transactions in the space given below.**

(i) James paid £20,000 into a business bank account in order to start his business.

Effect 1	Effect 2
▼	▼

Picklist:

Decrease in capital
Decrease in cash
Decrease in liabilities
Increase in cash
Increase in capital
Increase in liabilities (trade payables)

(ii) He paid an initial rental of £2,500 by cheque for the shop that he is to trade from.

Effect 1	Effect 2
▼	▼

Picklist:

Decrease in capital
Decrease in cash
Increase in assets
Increase in cash
Increase in liabilities (trade payables)
Rent expense incurred

(iii) He purchased a van by cheque for £7,400.

Effect 1	Effect 2
▼	▼

Picklist:

Decrease in capital
Decrease in cash
Decrease in liabilities (trade payables)
Increase in assets
Increase in cash
Van expense incurred

(iv) He purchased £6,000 of goods for resale on credit.

Effect 1	Effect 2
▼	▼

Picklist:

Decrease in cash
Decrease in liabilities (trade payables)
Increase in assets (trade receivables)
Increase in cash
Increase in liabilities (trade payables)
Increase in purchases

(v) He sold goods for £1,000 – the customer paid by cheque.

Effect 1	Effect 2
▼	▼

Picklist:

Decrease in cash
Decrease in purchases
Increase in assets (trade receivables)
Increase in cash
Increase in liabilities (trade payables)
Increase in sales

(vi) He sold goods on credit for £4,800.

Effect 1	Effect 2
▼	▼

Picklist:

Decrease in cash
Decrease in purchases
Increase in assets (trade receivables)
Increase in cash
Increase in liabilities (trade payables)
Increase in sales

(vii) He paid shop assistants' wages by cheque totalling £2,100.

Effect 1	Effect 2
▼	▼

Picklist:

Decrease in cash
Decrease in liabilities (trade payables)
Increase in cash
Increase in drawings
Increase in purchases
Wages expenses incurred

(viii) He made further sales on credit for £3,900.

Effect 1	Effect 2
▼	▼

Picklist:

Decrease in cash
Decrease in purchases
Increase in assets (trade receivables)
Increase in cash
Increase in liabilities (trade payables)
Increase in sales

(ix) He purchased a further £1,400 of goods for resale by cheque.

Effect 1	Effect 2
▼	▼

Picklist:

Decrease in cash
Decrease in liabilities (trade payables)
Increase in assets (trade receivables)
Increase in cash
Increase in liabilities (trade payables)
Increase in purchases

(x) £3,700 was received from credit customers.

Effect 1	Effect 2
▼	▼

Picklist:

Decrease in assets (trade receivables)
Decrease in liabilities (trade payables)
Decrease in sales
Increase in assets (trade receivables)
Increase in cash
Increase in purchases

(xi) He paid £3,300 to credit suppliers.

Effect 1	Effect 2
▼	▼

Picklist:

Decrease in assets (trade receivables)
Decrease in cash
Decrease in liabilities (trade payables)
Increase in assets (trade receivables)
Increase in cash
Increase in purchases

(xii) He withdrew £800 from the business for his living expenses.

Effect 1	Effect 2
▼	▼

Picklist:

Decrease in cash
Decrease in liabilities (trade payables)
Increase in cash
Increase in drawings
Increase in purchases
Wages expenses incurred

(b) **Enter James's transactions above in to his ledger accounts. You do not need to balance off the ledger accounts.**

Bank

Details	£	Details	£
▼		▼	
▼		▼	
▼		▼	
▼		▼	
▼		▼	
▼		▼	

Picklist:

Capital
Drawings
Purchases
Purchases ledger control
Sales
Sales ledger control
Rent
Van
Wages

Capital

Details		£	Details		£
	▼			▼	
	▼			▼	

Picklist:

Bank
Capital
Drawings
Purchases
Purchases ledger control
Sales
Sales ledger control
Rent
Van
Wages

Rent

Details		£	Details		£
	▼			▼	
	▼			▼	

Picklist:

Bank
Capital
Drawings
Purchases
Purchases ledger control
Sales
Sales ledger control
Rent
Van
Wages

Van

Details		£	Details		£
	▼			▼	
	▼			▼	

Picklist:

Bank
Capital
Drawings
Purchases
Purchases ledger control
Sales
Sales ledger control
Rent
Van
Wages

Purchases

Details	£	Details	£
▼		▼	
▼		▼	

Picklist:

Bank
Capital
Drawings
Purchases
Purchases ledger control
Sales
Sales ledger control
Rent
Van
Wages

Purchases ledger control

Details	£	Details	£
▼		▼	
▼		▼	

Picklist:

Bank
Capital
Drawings
Purchases
Purchases ledger control
Sales
Sales ledger control
Rent
Van
Wages

Sales account

Details		£	Details		£
	▼			▼	
	▼			▼	
	▼			▼	

Picklist:

Bank
Capital
Drawings
Purchases
Purchases ledger control
Sales
Sales ledger control
Rent
Van
Wages

Sales ledger control

Details		£	Details		£
	▼			▼	
	▼			▼	
	▼			▼	

Picklist:

Bank
Capital
Drawings
Purchases
Purchases ledger control
Sales
Sales ledger control
Rent
Van
Wages

Wages

Details		£	Details		£
	▼			▼	
	▼			▼	
	▼			▼	

Picklist:

Bank
Capital
Drawings
Purchases
Purchases ledger control
Sales
Sales ledger control
Rent
Van
Wages

Drawings

Details	£	Details	£
▼		▼	
▼		▼	
▼		▼	

Picklist:

Bank
Capital
Dawings
Purchases
Purchases ledger control
Sales
Sales ledger control
Rent
Van
Wages

Task 6.4

(a) **What is the double entry required for discounts allowed to customers?**

	Debit ✓	Credit ✓
Discounts allowed		
Sales ledger control		

(b) **What is the double entry required for discounts received from suppliers?**

	Debit ✓	Credit ✓
Discounts received		
Purchases ledger control		

(c) **What is the double entry required for a purchase of goods for resale made on credit?**

	Debit ✓	Credit ✓
Purchases		
Purchases ledger control		

(d) **What is the double entry required for a sale made on credit?**

	Debit ✓	Credit ✓
Sales		
Sales ledger control		

(e) **What is the double entry required for a sale made for cash?**

	Debit ✓	Credit ✓
Cash		
Sales		

(f) **What is the double entry required for cash received from a credit customer?**

	Debit ✓	Credit ✓
Cash		
Sales ledger control		

(g) **What is the double entry required for drawings made by the owner of a business?**

	Debit ✓	Credit ✓
Drawings		
Cash		

(h) **What is the double entry required for wages paid in cash to employees?**

	Debit ✓	Credit ✓
Wages		
Cash		

Chapter 7 Double entry bookkeeping (part 2)

Task 7.1

The following account is in the sales ledger of Smith & Co at the close of day on 31 May.

(a) **Insert the balance carried down together with date and details.**
(b) **Insert the totals.**
(c) **Insert the balance brought down together with date and details.**

TN Designs

Date 20XX	Details	Amount £	Date 20XX	Details	Amount £
1 May	Balance b/f	2,643	8 May	Bank	1,473
11 May	Invoice 27491	1,804	24 May	Credit note 381	265
18 May	Invoice 27513	1,088			
▼	▼		▼	▼	
	Total			Total	
▼	▼		▼	▼	

Picklist:

31 May
1 June
Balance b/d
Balance c/d
Smith & Co
T N Designs

Task 7.2

The following account is in the purchases ledger of Smith & Co at the close of day on 30 September.

(a) **Insert the balance carried down together with date and details.**
(b) **Insert the totals.**
(c) **Insert the balance brought down together with date and details.**

Harold & Partners

Date 20XX	Details	Amount £	Date 20XX	Details	Amount £
7 Sept	Bank	635	1 Sept	Balance b/f	1,367
7 Sept	Discount	33	5 Sept	Invoice 27465	998
30 Sept	Credit note 364	106	12 Sept	Invoice 27499	478
▼	▼		▼	▼	
	Total			Total	
▼	▼		▼	▼	

Picklist:

30 Sept
1 Oct
Balance b/d
Balance c/d
Smith & Co
Harold & Partners

Task 7.3

A payment is made to a supplier for £367.48 after a prompt payment discount of £12.50 has been taken.

What is the double entry for this transaction?

Account name		Debit £	Credit £
	▼		
	▼		
	▼		

Picklist:

Bank
Discount allowed
Discount received
Purchases
Purchases ledger control
Sales
Sales ledger control

Task 7.4

For each of the following, indicate whether they are capital or revenue transactions:

	Capital ✓	Revenue ✓
Purchase of a new computer paid for by cheque		
Purchase of printer paper by cheque		
Purchase of a new business car on credit		
Payment of road tax on a new business car		
Payment of rent for the business premises		

Task 7.5

For the following ledger accounts, you are required to.

(a) Insert the balance carried down together with date and details.
(b) Insert the totals.
(c) Insert the balance brought down together with date and details.

Purchases ledger control

Date	Details	£	Date	Details	£
31 Oct	Purchases returns	4,467	1 Oct	Balance b/d	41,204
31 Oct	Bank	36,409	31 Oct	Purchases	52,390
31 Oct	Discounts received	125			
▼	▼		▼	▼	
	Total			Total	
▼	▼		▼	▼	

Picklist:

31 Oct
1 Nov
Balance b/d
Balance c/d
Purchases ledger control
Petty cash
VAT

Petty cash

Date	Details	£	Date	Details	£
1 Oct	Balance b/d	200.00	31 Oct	Expenses	183.25
31 Oct	Bank	183.25			
▼	▼		▼	▼	
	Total			Total	
▼	▼		▼	▼	

Picklist:

31 Oct
1 Nov
Balance b/d
Balance c/d
Petty cash
Purchases ledger control
VAT

VAT

Date	Details	£	Date	Details	£
31 Oct	Sales returns	40.00	1 Oct	Balance b/d	183.25
31 Oct	Purchases	1,900.00	31 Oct	Purchases returns	62.00
			31 Oct	Sales	3,250.00
▼	▼		▼	▼	
	Total			Total	
▼	▼		▼	▼	

Picklist:

31 Oct
1 Nov
Balance b/d
Balance c/d
Petty cash
Purchases ledger control
VAT

Task 7.6

For each of the following, indicate whether they are capital or revenue transactions:

	Capital ✓	Revenue ✓
Payment of a credit supplier for goods received for resale		
Receipt of proceeds from sale of car used in the business		
Payment of drawings to the business owner		
Acquisition of new machine for use over five years		
Payment by a cash customer for goods		

Task 7.7

The following two accounts are in the general ledger at the close of day on 30 November.

(a) Insert the balance carried down together with date and details.
(b) Insert the totals.
(c) Insert the balance brought down together with date and details.

Purchases

Date 20XX	Details	Amount £	Date 20XX	Details	Amount £
01 Nov	Balance b/d	140,389		▼	
15 Nov	Purchases ledger control	14,388		▼	
30 Nov	Purchases ledger control	52,389		▼	
	▼			▼	
	Total			Total	
	▼			▼	

Picklist:

Balance b/d
Balance c/d
Bank
Purchases
Purchases ledger control
Sales ledger control

Bank interest received

Date 20XX	Details	Amount £	Date 20XX	Details	Amount £
	▼		01 Nov	Balance b/d	32
	▼		15 Nov	Bank	14
	▼		30 Nov	Bank	22
	▼			▼	
	Total			Total	
	▼			▼	

Picklist:

Balance b/d
Balance c/d
Bank
Bank interest received
Purchases ledger control
Sales ledger control

Task 7.8

It is important to understand the difference between capital expenditure, revenue expenditure, capital income and revenue income.

Select one option in each instance below to show whether the item will be capital expenditure, revenue expenditure, capital income or revenue income.

Item	Capital expenditure ✓	Revenue expenditure ✓	Capital income ✓	Revenue income ✓
Payment in advance for 3 months of phone line rental				
Proceeds from sale of machinery				
Sale of suitcases for cash				
Receipt of payment from trade receivable for bags				
Purchase of a shop building				
Petty cash payment for stationery				

Task 7.9

For each of the items below, identify an example from the picklist provided.

Item	Example	
Asset		▼
Liability		▼
Capital transaction		▼

Picklist:

Bank overdraft
Drawings
Trade receivables

Chapter 8 Maintaining the cash book

Task 8.1

There are four payments to be entered in the credit side of Natural Production's cash book during one week.

Cash purchases listing

Suppliers paid in cash	Net £	VAT £	Gross £
Mendip plc	115	23	138

Trade payables listing

Credit suppliers paid by cheque	Amount paid £
W J Jones	521
Trenter Ltd	358
Packing Supplies	754

(a) **Enter the details from the cash purchases listing and the trade payables listing into the credit side of the cash book shown below and total each column.**

Details	Cash £	Bank £	VAT £	Cash purchases £	Trade payables £
Balance b/f		735			
▼					
▼					
▼					
▼					
Total					

Picklist:

Bank
Cash
Cash purchases
Mendip plc
Packing Supplies
Trade payables
Trenter Ltd
VAT
W J Jones

The debit side of the cash book shows the cash balance brought forward at the beginning of the week was £200 and a further £319 has been received during the week.

(b) Using your answer to (a) above, calculate the cash balance.

£ [   ]

The debit side of the cash book shows the total amount of money banked during the week was £560.

(c) Using your answer to (a) above, calculate the bank balance. If your calculations show that the bank account is overdrawn, your answer should start with a minus sign, for example –123.

£ [   ]

(d) Is the balance at bank calculated in (c) above a debit or a credit balance?

	✓
Debit	
Credit	

Task 8.2

Given below are the cheque stubs for the two payments made by Newmans on 27 January.

You have also looked at the standing order and direct debit instruction file and noted that there is a standing order due to be paid to the local council for business rates of £255 on the 27th of each month, and a direct debit for rent of £500 also due on 27th of the month.

Cheque book stubs

Henson Press	Ely Instruments
(Purchases ledger account HEN006)	(Purchases ledger account ELY003)
£329	£736
000168	000169

Make the necessary entries in the cash book and total each column.

Cash book – credit side

Details		Cash £	Bank £	VAT £	Trade payables £	Cash purchases £	Rent & rates £
	▼						
	▼						
	▼						
	▼						
Total							

Picklist:

Cash purchases
Ely Instruments
Henson Press
Newmans
Rates
Rent
Trade payables

Task 8.3

The two amounts shown below have been received from customers and are ready to be entered in the cash book.

Receipt 56
11 July 20XX
Cheque for £500 and cash £334 received from Hoppers Ltd plc for goods supplied today – £834 including VAT.

Body Perfect Remittance advice
13 July 20XX
An amount of £542 will be transferred to your bank account today by BACS, in full settlement of our May account.

Make the necessary entries in the cash book and total each column.

Cash book – debit side

Details	Cash £	Bank £	VAT £	Trade receivables £	Cash sales £
Balance b/f	120	1,520			
▼					
▼					
Totals					

Picklist:

Bank
Body Perfect
Cash
Hoppers Ltd
Trade receivables
VAT

Task 8.4

The two amounts shown below have been received from customers and are ready to be entered in the cash book.

Receipt 56
14 Oct 20XX
Cash £210 received from Howsham Ltd plc for goods supplied today – £210 including VAT.

Esporta Leisure Remittance advice
14 Oct 20XX
Please find enclosed a cheque for £958 in full settlement of invoice 2457.

Make the necessary entries in the cash book and total each column.

Cash book – debit side

Details	Cash £	Bank £	VAT £	Trade receivables £	Cash sales £
Balance b/f	56	1,805			
▼					
▼					
Totals					

Picklist:

Bank
Cash
Esporta Leisure
Howsham Ltd
Trade receivables
VAT

....

Task 8.5

There are five payments to be entered in Canlan Ltd's cash book.

Receipts from suppliers for Canlan Ltd's cash purchases

| **Supplier: Dubai Dreams**

Received cash with thanks for goods bought.

Net   £270
VAT   £54
Total   £324 | **Supplier: Walter Enterprises**

Received cash with thanks for goods bought.

Net   £190
VAT   £38
Total   £228 | **Supplier: Sinead Reilly**

Received cash with thanks for goods bought.

Net   £56
(No VAT) |

Stubs from Canlan Ltd's cheque book

| Payee: Sumatra Trading
(Purchases ledger account PL026)

£7,265

Cheque number 093673 | Payee: SHSK Co
For stationery
(Canlan Ltd has no credit account with this supplier)

£378 including VAT

Cheque number 093674 |

(a) **Enter the details of the three receipts from suppliers and two cheque book stubs into the credit side of the cash book shown below. Total each column.**

Cash book – credit side

Details	Cash £	Bank £	VAT £	Trade payables £	Cash purchases £	Stationery £
Balance b/f		236				
Dubai Dreams						
Walter Enterprises						
Sinead Reilly						
Sumatra Trading						
SHSK Co						
Total						

(b) There are two cheques from credit customers to be entered in the cash book:

Park Farm Stores £2,576

Tristram Pale Ltd £4,233

Enter these details into the debit side of the cash book and total each column.

Cash book – debit side

Details	Cash £	Bank £	VAT £	Trade receivables £
Balance b/f	1,228			
Park Farm Stores				
Tristram Pale Ltd				
Total				

(c) **Using your answers to (a) and (b) above, calculate the cash balance.**

£

(d) **Using your answers to (a) and (b) above, calculate the bank balance.**

£

(e) **Is the bank balance calculated in (d) above a debit or credit balance?**

	✓
Debit	
Credit	

Task 8.6

There are five payments to be entered in Kitchen Kuts' cash book.

Receipts

<table>
<tr>
<td>

Received cash with thanks for goods bought.

From Kitchen Kuts, a customer without a credit account.

Net   £200
VAT   £40
Total £240

B Smithson Ltd

</td>
<td>

Received cash with thanks for goods bought.

From Kitchen Kuts, a customer without a credit account.

Net   £160
VAT   £32
Total £192

H Hamnet

</td>
<td>

Received cash with thanks for goods bought.

From Kitchen Kuts, a customer without a credit account.

Net   £320
(No VAT)

Renee Reid

</td>
</tr>
</table>

Cheque book stubs

<table>
<tr>
<td>

Tenon Ltd
(Purchase ledger account TEN006)

£3,600

000168

</td>
<td>

Vernon Motor Repairs
(We have no credit account with this supplier)

£48 including VAT

000169

</td>
</tr>
</table>

(a) Enter the details from the three receipts and two cheque book stubs into the credit side of the cash book shown below and total each column.

Cash book – credit side

Details	Cash £	Bank £	VAT £	Trade payables £	Cash purchases £	Motor expenses £
Balance b/f		16,942				
B Smithson Ltd						
H Hamnet						
Renee Reid						
Tenon Ltd						
Vernon Motor Repairs						
Total						

There are two cheques from credit customers to be entered in Kitchen Kuts' cash book:

G Brownlow   £749
S Barnett   £300

(b) Enter the above details into the debit side of the cash book and total each column.

Cash book – debit side

Details	Cash £	Bank £	VAT £	Trade receivables £
Balance b/f	1,325			
G Brownlow				
S Barnett				
Total				

(c) Using your answers to (a) and (b) above, calculate the cash balance.

£ [   ]

(d) Using your answers to (a) and (b) above, calculate the bank balance.

£ [   ]

(e) Will the bank balance calculated in (d) above be a debit or credit balance?

	✓
Debit	
Credit	

Task 8.7

Shown below are the debit and credit sides of Halliday Ltd's cash book.

You are required to balance off Halliday Ltd's cash book.

Cash book – debit side

Details	Cash £	Bank £	VAT £	Trade receivables £	Cash sales £
Balance b/f	55	1,300			
Whippet's	210		35		175
Ragdoll Ltd		958		958	
▼					
Totals					
▼					

Picklist:

Balance b/d
Balance c/d
Halliday Ltd
Ragdoll Ltd
Whippet's

Cash book – credit side

Details	Cash £	Bank £	VAT £	Trade payables £	Cash purchases £
Hornsea Ltd		355		355	
Lyndon Plc		738		738	
▼					
Total					
▼					

Picklist:
Balance b/d
Balance c/d
Halliday Ltd
Ragdoll Ltd
Whippet's

Task 8.8

There are three receipts to be entered in the debit side of the cash-book during one week.

Cash sales listing

Sale made for cash	Net £	VAT £	Gross £
Humber & Co	485	97	582

Trade receivables listing

Credit customers paying by cheque	Amount paid £
Ridgely Ltd	2,150
Watts Partners	978

(a) **Enter the details from the cash sales listing and the trade receivables listing into the debit side of the cash-book shown below and total each column.**

Cash book – debit side

Details	Cash £	Bank £	VAT £	Trade receivables £	Cash sales £
Balance b/f	159	844			
Humber & Co					
Ridgely Ltd					
Watts Partners					
Total					

The credit side of the cash-book shows cash spent on cash purchases of £561 during the week.

(b) **Using your answer to (a) above, calculate the cash balance.**

£ [   ]

The credit side of the cash-book shows the total amount of cheques sent during the week was £4,085.

(c) **Using your answer to (a) above, calculate the bank balance. If your calculations show that the bank account is overdrawn, your answer should start with a minus sign, for example –123.**

£ [   ]

Chapter 9 Double entry for sales and trade receivables

Task 9.1

The following credit transactions have been entered into the sales day book as shown below. No entries have yet been made into the ledgers.

Sales day book

Date 20XX	Customer	Invoice number	Customer code	Total £	VAT £	Net £
Dec	S Himms	00011	SL 18	900	150	750
Dec	G Pood	00012	SL 13	1,500	250	1,250
Dec	M Kitchell	00013	SL 04	456	76	380
Dec	B Crown	00014	SL 15	1,392	232	1,160
Totals				4,248	708	3,540

(a) **What will be the entries in the sales ledger?**

Sales ledger

Account name		Amount £	Debit ✓	Credit ✓
	▼			
	▼			
	▼			
	▼			

Picklist:

B Crown
G Pood
M Kitchell
Purchases
Purchases ledger control
Purchases returns
S Himms
Sales
Sales ledger control
Sales returns
VAT

(b) **What will be the entries in the general ledger?**

General ledger

Account name		Amount £	Debit ✓	Credit ✓
	▼			
	▼			
	▼			

Picklist:

B Crown
G Pood
M Kitchell
Purchases
Purchases ledger control
Purchases returns
S Himms
Sales
Sales ledger control
Sales returns
VAT

Task 9.2

The following credit transactions have been entered into the sales day book as shown below. No entries have yet been made into the ledgers.

Sales day book

Date 20XX	Customer	Invoice number	Customer code	Total £	VAT £	Net £
Jan	H Simms	0001	SL 45	1,800	300	1,500
Jan	P Good	0002	SL 21	3,000	500	2,500
Jan	K Mitchell	0003	SL 30	912	152	760
Jan	C Brown	0004	SL 05	2,790	465	2,325
Totals				8,502	1,417	7,085

(a) Post these transactions to the general ledger accounts shown below.

General ledger

Sales ledger control

Details		£	Details		£
	▼			▼	
	▼			▼	
	▼			▼	

Picklist:
Bank
Cash
C Brown
H Simms
K Mitchell
P Good
Purchases
Purchases ledger control
Sales
Sales ledger control
VAT

Sales

Details		£	Details		£
	▼			▼	
	▼			▼	

Picklist:
Bank
Cash
C Brown
H Simms
K Mitchell
P Good
Purchases
Purchases ledger control
Sales
Sales ledger control
VAT

VAT

Details		£	Details		£
	▼			▼	
	▼			▼	

Picklist:

Bank
Cash
H Simms
K Mitchell
Sales
Sales ledger control
VAT

(b) **Post the transactions with H Simms and K Mitchell to the relevant accounts in the Sales ledger.**

Sales ledger

H Simms SL45

Details		£	Details		£
	▼			▼	

Picklist:

Bank
Cash
H Simms
K Mitchell
Sales day book
Sales ledger control

K Mitchell SL 30

Details		£	Details		£
	▼			▼	

Picklist:

Bank
Cash
H Simms
K Mitchell
Sales day book
Sales ledger control

Task 9.3

The following credit transactions have been entered into Natural Production's sales day book as shown below. No entries have yet been made into the ledgers.

Sales day book

Date 20XX	Customer	Invoice number	Total £	VAT £	Net £
2 Jan	Hoppers Ltd	6237	656.40	109.40	547.00
5 Jan	Body Perfect	6238	744.00	124.00	620.00
			1,400.40	233.40	1,167.00

(a) **What will be the entries in the sales ledger?**

Sales ledger

Account name	Amount £	Debit ✓	Credit ✓
▼			
▼			

Picklist:

Body Perfect
Hoppers Ltd
Natural Productions
Purchases returns
Sales
Sales ledger control
Sales returns
VAT

(b) **What will be the entries in the general ledger?**

General ledger

Account name	Amount £	Debit ✓	Credit ✓
▼			
▼			
▼			

Picklist:

Body Perfect
Hoppers Ltd
Natural Productions
Purchases
Purchases ledger control
Purchases returns
Sales
Sales ledger control
Sales returns
VAT

Task 9.4

The following credit transactions have been entered into Natural Production's sales day book as shown below. No entries have yet been made into the ledgers.

Sales day book

Date 20XX	Customer	Invoice number	Total £	VAT £	Net £
21 Jan	Esporta Leisure	6239	415.20	69.20	346.00
25 Jan	Langans Beauty	6240	273.60	45.60	228.00
			688.80	114.80	574.00

(a) **Post the totals of the sales day book to the general ledger accounts given.**

General ledger

Sales ledger control

Details	£	Details	£
▼		▼	
▼		▼	
▼		▼	

Picklist:

Bank
Cash
Esporta Leisure
Langans Beauty
Purchases
Purchases ledger control
Sales
Sales ledger control
VAT

Sales

Details		£	Details		£
	▼			▼	
	▼			▼	

Picklist:

Bank
Cash
Esporta Leisure
Langans Beauty
Purchases
Purchases ledger control
Sales
Sales ledger control
VAT

VAT

Details		£	Details		£
	▼			▼	
	▼			▼	

Picklist:

Bank
Cash
Esporta Leisure
Langans Beauty
Sales
Sales ledger control
VAT

(b) Post the individual entries to the sales ledger.

Sales ledger

Langans Beauty

Details		£	Details		£
	▼			▼	

Picklist:

Bank
Cash
Esporta Leisure
Langans Beauty
Sales day book
Sales ledger control

Esporta Leisure

Details		£	Details		£
	▼			▼	

Picklist:

Bank
Cash
Esporta Leisure
Langans Beauty
Sales day book

Task 9.5

The following credit transactions have been entered into Short Furniture's sales day book as shown below. No entries have yet been made into the ledgers.

Sales day book

Customer	Invoice number	Customer code	Invoice total £	VAT £	Net £
Rocks Garden Suppliers	08663	SL22	701.76	116.96	584.80
Eridge Nurseries	08664	SL07	429.30	71.55	357.75
Abergaven GC	08665	SL16	923.40	153.90	769.50
Rother Nurseries	08666	SL13	756.00	126.00	630.00
			2,810.46	468.41	2,342.05

(a) What will be the entries in the sales ledger?

Sales ledger

Account name		Amount £	Debit ✓	Credit ✓
	▼			
	▼			
	▼			
	▼			

Picklist:

Abergaven GC
Eridge Nurseries
Purchases returns
Rocks Garden Suppliers
Rother Nurseries
Sales
Sales ledger control
Sales returns
Short Furniture
VAT

(b) What will be the entries in the general ledger?

General ledger

Account name	Amount £	Debit ✓	Credit ✓
▼			
▼			
▼			

Picklist:

Abergaven GC
Eridge Nurseries
Purchases returns
Rocks Garden Suppliers
Rother Nurseries
Sales
Sales ledger control
Sales returns
Short Furniture
VAT

Task 9.6

During January, Natural Productions issued some credit notes as shown in the sales returns day book below. No entries have yet been made into the ledgers.

Sales returns day book

Date 20XX	Customer	Credit note number	Total £	VAT £	Net £
17 Jan	Hoppers Ltd	1476	82.44	13.74	68.70
23 Jan	Esporta Leisure	1477	107.04	17.84	89.20
30 Jan	Superior Products	1478	14.16	2.36	11.80
			203.64	33.94	169.70

(a) **What will be the entries in the sales ledger?**

Sales ledger

Account name		Amount £	Debit ✓	Credit ✓
	▼			
	▼			
	▼			

Picklist:

Esporta Leisure
Hoppers Ltd
Natural Productions
Purchases
Purchases ledger control
Purchases returns
Sales
Sales ledger control
Sales returns
Superior Products
VAT

(b) **What will be the entries in the general ledger?**

General ledger

Account name		Amount £	Debit ✓	Credit ✓
	▼			
	▼			
	▼			

Picklist:

Esporta Leisure
Hoppers Ltd
Natural Productions
Purchases
Purchases ledger control
Purchases returns
Sales
Sales ledger control
Sales returns
Superior Products
VAT

Task 9.7

Natural Productions discounts allowed day book is shown below. No entries have yet been made into the ledgers.

Discounts allowed day book

Date 20XX	Customer	Credit note number	Total £	VAT £	Net £
1 Feb	Hoppers Ltd	1501	36	6	30
25 Feb	Esporta Leisure	1502	72	12	60
			108	18	90

(a) **What will be the entries in the sales ledger?**

Sales ledger

Account name		Amount £	Debit ✓	Credit ✓
	▼			
	▼			

Picklist:

Discounts allowed
Discounts received
Esporta Leisure
Hoppers Ltd
Purchases
Purchases ledger control
Purchases returns
Sales
Sales ledger control
Sales returns
VAT

(b) What will be the entries in the general ledger?

General ledger

Account name		Amount £	Debit ✓	Credit ✓
	▼			
	▼			
	▼			

Picklist:

Discounts allowed
Discounts received
Purchases
Purchases ledger control
Purchases returns
Sales
Sales ledger control
Sales returns
VAT

Task 9.8

You work for Short Furniture. A remittance advice and cheque for £1,112.17 has been received from Rother Nurseries which they state is in full settlement of the account at 31 January. The remittance advice and the customer's account in the sales ledger is shown below.

Rother Nurseries		
REMITTANCE ADVICE		
To: Short Furniture		Date: 1 Feb 20XX
Please find attached our cheque for full settlement of our account as at 31 January 20XX		

Invoice number	Credit note number	Amount £
08666		756.00
08674		114.78
	1470	(96.50)
08681		337.89
Total amount paid		**£1,112.17**

Sales ledger

Rother Nurseries   SL 16

Date	Details	£	Date	Details	£
9 Jan	Invoice 08666	756.00	20 Jan	Credit note 1470	96.50
16 Jan	Invoice 08674	214.78			
24 Jan	Invoice 08681	337.89			
5 Feb	Invoice 08695	265.98			

(a)   **Check the remittance advice against the customer's account in the sales ledger and state whether the following statements are true or false.**

	True ✓	False ✓
Rother Nurseries has fully settled their account at 31 January 20XX.		
Rother Nurseries should have included invoice 08695 with their payment in order to fully settle their account at 31 January.		
The remittance advice note has been correctly cast.		
The invoice amounts are included correctly on the remittance advice note.		

(b) What amount should Rother Nurseries have paid to fully settle their account as at 31 January?

£ [   ]

Task 9.9

A remittance advice and cheque for £2,279.30 has been received from Abergaven Garden Centre which they state is in full settlement of the account at 9 February. The remittance advice and the customer's account in the sales ledger is shown below.

Abergaven Garden Centre
REMITTANCE ADVICE

To: Short Furniture   Date: 9 Feb 20XX

Please find attached our cheque for full settlement of our account as at 31 January 20XX

Invoice number	Credit note number	Amount £
08665		923.40
08672		623.56
08685		316.58
08692		415.76
Total amount paid		£1,863.54

Abergaven Garden Centre   **SL 17**

Date	Details	£	Date	Details	£
7 Jan	Invoice 08665	923.40	13 Jan	Credit note 1471	32.50
13 Jan	Invoice 08672	623.56	2 Feb	Credit note 1476	110.23
26 Jan	Invoice 08685	316.58			
3 Feb	Invoice 08692	415.76			

(a) Check the remittance advice against the customer's account in the sales ledger and state whether the following statements are true or false.

	True ✓	False ✓
Abergaven Garden Centre has included on the remittance advice note all relevant transactions up to 9 February.		
The remittance advice note has been correctly cast.		
The invoice amounts are included correctly on the remittance advice note.		

(b) **What amount should Abergaven Garden Centre have paid to fully settle their account as at 9 February?**

£	

Task 9.10

Shown below are the totals of Natural Productions' cash book – debit side, at the end of the week.

Cash book – debit side

Date	Details	Cash £	Bank £	VAT £	Cash sales £	Trade receivables £
		279.84	2,018.10	46.64	233.20	2,018.10

What will be the entries in the general ledger?

Account name	Amount £	Debit ✓	Credit ✓
▼			
▼			
▼			

Picklist:

Bank
Cash
Cash purchases
Cash sales
Purchases ledger control
Sales ledger control
VAT

Task 9.11

Natural Productions' cash book – debit side, is shown below. The cash book is not part of the general ledger.

Date	Details	Cash £	Bank £	VAT £	Cash sales £	Trade receivables £
23 Jan	Hoppers Ltd		553.96			553.96
23 Jan	Superior Products		116.70			116.70
24 Jan	Cash sales	131.16		21.86	109.30	
25 Jan	Esporta Leisure		367.20			367.20
27 Jan	Cash sales	88.56		14.76	73.80	
27 Jan	Body Perfect		706.64			706.64
27 Jan	Cash sales	60.12		10.02	50.10	
27 Jan	Langans Beauty		273.60			273.60
		279.84	2,018.10	46.64	233.20	2,018.10

(a) **Post the entries to the individual accounts in the sales ledger shown below.**

Sales ledger

Hoppers Ltd

Details	£	Details	£
Invoice 6237	656.40	Credit note 1476	82.44
▼		▼	

Picklist:

Bank
Cash sales
Hoppers Ltd
Natural Productions
Purchases
Purchases ledger control
Sales
Sales ledger control
Trade receivables
VAT

Body Perfect

Details	£		£
Invoice 6238	744.00		

Picklist:

Bank
Body Perfect
Cash sales
Natural Productions
Purchases
Purchases ledger control
Sales
Sales ledger control
Trade receivables
VAT

Esporta Leisure

Details	£	Details	£
Invoice 6239	415.20	Credit note 1477	107.04

Picklist:

Bank
Cash sales
Esporta Leisure
Natural Productions
Purchases
Purchases ledger control
Sales
Sales ledger control
Trade receivables
VAT

Langans Beauty

Details	£	Details	£
Invoice 6240	273.60		

Picklist:

Bank
Cash sales
Langans Beauty
Natural Productions
Purchases
Purchases ledger control
Sales
Sales ledger control
Trade receivables
VAT

Superior Products

Details	£	Details	£
Invoice 6242	265.20	Credit note 1478	14.16
▼			▼	

Picklist:

Bank
Cash sales
Natural Productions
Purchases
Purchases ledger control
Sales
Sales ledger control
Superior Products
Trade receivables
VAT

(b) **Post the totals to the general ledger accounts shown below.**

General ledger

Cash

Details	£	Details	£
▼		▼	
▼		▼	

Picklist

Bank
Body Perfect
Cash
Esporta Leisure
Hoppers Ltd
Langans Beauty
Sales
Sales ledger control
Superior Products
VAT

Bank

Details		£	Details		£
	▽			▽	
	▽			▽	

Picklist

Bank
Body Perfect
Cash
Esporta Leisure
Hoppers Ltd
Langans Beauty
Sales
Sales ledger control
Superior Products
VAT

Sales ledger control

Details		£	Details		£
Sales		3,438.00	Sales returns		169.70
VAT		687.60	VAT		33.94
	▽			▽	
	▽			▽	

Picklist

Bank
Body Perfect
Cash
Esporta Leisure
Hoppers Ltd
Langans Beauty
Sales
Sales ledger control
Superior Products
VAT

Sales

Details		£	Details		£
	▽		Sales ledger control		3,438.00
	▽			▽	

Picklist

Bank
Body Perfect
Cash
Esporta Leisure
Hoppers Ltd
Langans Beauty
Sales
Sales ledger control
Superior Products
VAT

VAT

Details	£	Details	£
Sales ledger control	33.94	Sales ledger control	687.60
▼		▼	

Picklist

Bank
Body Perfect
Cash
Esporta Leisure
Hoppers Ltd
Langans Beauty
Sales
Sales ledger control
Superior Products
VAT

Task 9.12

The following transactions all took place on 30 June and have been entered in the debit side of the cash book as shown below. No entries have yet been made in the ledgers.

Cash book – debit side

Date 20XX	Details	Cash £	Bank £	VAT £	Cash sales £	Trade receivables £
30 Jun	Henderson & Co		7,349			7,349
30 Jun	Cash sale	426		71	355	

BPP
LEARNING MEDIA

(a) **What will be the entry in the sales ledger?**

Sales ledger

Account name		Amount £	Debit ✓	Credit ✓
	▼			

Picklist:

Bank
Cash
Henderson & Co
Purchases ledger control
Sales
Sales ledger control
VAT

(b) **What will be the three entries in the general ledger?**

General ledger

Account name		Amount £	Debit ✓	Credit ✓
	▼			
	▼			
	▼			

Picklist:

Bank
Cash
Henderson & Co
Purchases ledger control
Sales
Sales ledger control
VAT

Task 9.13

You work in the accounts department of Southfield Electrical. The following are extracts from the day books relating to transactions in May 20XX with Alpha Services & Co. together with a remittance advice note for a cheque payment received in May 20XX from the customer.

Sales day book – extract

Date 20XX	Customer	Invoice number	Customer code	Total £	VAT £	Net £
7 May	Alpha Services	715	SL10	5,190.00	865.00	4,325.00
17 May	Alpha Services	787	SL10	10,020.00	1,670.00	8,350.00

Sales returns day book – extract

Date 20XX	Customer	Credit note number	Customer code	Total £	VAT £	Net £
12 May	Alpha Services	551	SL10	624.00	104.00	520.00

REMITTANCE ADVICE NOTE Alpha Services	Remittance advice note number 013278
Supplier:	Southfield Electrical
Account number (supplier code)	PL 821

Date	Transaction reference	Amount £
21/04/XX	Invoice 600	289.50
27/04/XX	Credit note 401	(35.87)
1/5/XX	Payment made – cheque enclosed	253.63

(a) Enter the transactions from the day books and the remittance advice in to the customer's account in the sales ledger. You do not need to balance off the account.

Sales ledger

Alpha Services

SL 10

Details	£	Details		£
Balance b/d	253.63		▼	
	▼			▼	
	▼			▼	
	▼			▼	

Picklist:
Alpha Services
Bank
Cash sales
Invoice 715
Invoice 787
Credit note 551
Purchases
Purchases ledger control
Sales
Sales ledger control
Southfield Electrical
Trade receivables
VAT

(b) **Using the information from part (a) complete the statement of account for Alpha Services below by:**

- **Entering the amount of the balance brought forward into the final column**
- **Writing the individual date and details below into the first column**
- **Entering the outstanding amount after every transaction into the final column**

STATEMENT OF ACCOUNT
Southfield Electrical
Industrial Estate
Benham DR6 2FF

To: Alpha Services   Date: 31 May 20XX

Date and details	Transaction amount £	Outstanding amount £
1 May – Balance b/f		
	253.63	
	5,190.00	
	624.00	
	10,020.00	

Date and details:

2 May - Payment received	7 May – Invoice 715	12 May - Credit note 551

17 May - Invoice 787

Task 9.14

The following transactions all took place on 30 November and have been entered into the sales day book as shown below. No entries have yet been made into the ledger system.

Sales day book

Date 20XX	Details	Invoice number	Total £	VAT @ 20% £	Net £
30 Nov	Gringles Co	12786	300	50	250
30 Nov	Lester plc	12787	1,308	218	1,090
30 Nov	Shrier Goods	12788	2,676	446	2,230
30 Nov	Abunda Bags	12789	1,992	332	1,660
	Totals		6,276	1,046	5,230

(a) **What will be the entries in the sales ledger?**

Sales ledger

Account name		Amount £	Debit ✓	Credit ✓
	▼			
	▼			
	▼			
	▼			

Picklist:

Abunda Bags
Gringles Co
Lester plc
Purchases
Purchases ledger control
Purchases returns
Sales
Sales ledger control
Sales returns
Shrier Goods
VAT

(b) **What will be the entries in the general ledger?**

General ledger

Account name		Amount £	Debit ✓	Credit ✓
	▼			
	▼			
	▼			

Picklist:

Abunda Bags
Gringles Co
Lester plc
Purchases
Purchases ledger control
Purchases returns
Sales
Sales ledger control
Sales returns
Shrier Goods
VAT

Chapter 10 Double entry for purchases and trade payables

Task 10.1

You have been given an extract from your organisation's purchases day book in respect of credit transactions in June. No entries have yet been made in the ledgers.

(a) Complete and total the purchases day book shown below.

Purchases day book

Date 20XX	Details	Invoice number	Total £	VAT £	Net £
30 June	Seashell Ltd	8971			3,211.00
30 June	Opal & Co	05119	4,800.00		
	Totals				

(b) Using your answer from (a) above, record the transactions in the purchases ledger.

Purchases ledger

Account name		Amount £	Debit ✓	Credit ✓
	▼			
	▼			

Picklist:

Net
Opal & Co
Purchases
Purchases ledger control
Purchases returns
Sales
Sales ledger control
Sales returns
Seashell Ltd
Total
VAT

Task 10.2

These are the totals of the purchases day book at the end of the month.

Purchases day book

Details	Total £	VAT £	Net £	Purchases £	Stationery £	Packaging £
Totals	4,148.40	691.40	3,457.00	2,711.00	314.00	432.00

(a) **What will be the entries in the general ledger?**

Account name	Amount £	Debit ✓	Credit ✓
▼			
▼			
▼			
▼			
▼			

Picklist:

Packaging
Purchases
Purchases ledger control
Purchases returns
Sales
Sales ledger control
Sales returns
Stationery
VAT

One of the entries in the purchases day book is for an invoice from W J Jones for £210 plus VAT.

(b) **What will be the entry in the purchases ledger?**

Account name	Amount £	Debit ✓	Credit ✓
▼			

Picklist:

Discounts allowed
Discounts received
Purchases
Purchases ledger control
Purchases returns
Sales
Sales ledger control
Sales returns
VAT
W J Jones

Task 10.3

Natural Productions' purchases day book is shown below.

Purchases day book

Date	Supplier	Invoice number	Total £	VAT £	Net £	Purchases £	Packaging £
31 Jan	P J Phillips	03576	428.40	71.40	357.00	357.00	
31 Jan	Packing Supplies Ltd	28423	321.60	53.60	268.00		268.00
			750.00	125.00	625.00	357.00	268.00

(a) Post the totals of the purchases day book to the general ledger accounts given.

General ledger

Purchases ledger control

Details		£	Details		£
	▼			▼	
	▼			▼	
	▼			▼	

Picklist:

Packing Supplies Ltd
PJ Phillips
Purchases
Purchases ledger control
Purchases returns
Sales
Sales ledger control
Sales returns
VAT

VAT

Details		£	Details		£
	▼			▼	
	▼			▼	

Picklist:

Packing Supplies Ltd
PJ Phillips
Purchases
Purchases ledger control
Purchases returns
Sales
Sales ledger control
Sales returns
VAT

Purchases

Details		£	Details		£
	▼			▼	
	▼			▼	

Picklist:

Packing Supplies Ltd
PJ Phillips
Purchases
Purchases ledger control
Purchases returns
Sales
Sales ledger control
Sales returns
VAT

Packaging

Details		£	Details		£
	▼			▼	
	▼			▼	

Picklist:

Packing Supplies Ltd
PJ Phillips
Purchases
Purchases ledger control
Purchases returns
Sales
Sales ledger control
Sales returns
VAT

(b) **Post the individual entries to the purchases ledger accounts given.**

Purchases ledger

P J Phillips

Details		£	Details		£
	▼			▼	

Picklist:

Packing Supplies Ltd
PJ Phillips
Purchases day book
Purchases returns day book
VAT

Packing Supplies Ltd

Details	£	Details	£
▼		▼	

Picklist:

Packing Supplies Ltd
PJ Phillips
Purchases day book
Purchases returns day book
VAT

Task 10.4

Given below is Short Furniture's purchases day book as at 27 January.

Purchases day book

Date	Supplier	Invoice number	Supplier code	Total £	VAT £	Net £	Wood purchases £	Polish/ varnish purchases £	Other purchases £
27 Jan	Ephraim Supplies	09642	PL39	349.20	58.20	291.00	291.00		
27 Jan	Cavendish Woods	06932	PL14	846.12	141.02	705.10	705.10		
27 Jan	Calverley Bros	67671	PL03	174.72	29.12	145.60		145.60	
27 Jan	Culverden & Co	36004	PL23	68.88	11.48	57.40			57.40
				1,438.92	239.82	1,199.10	996.10	145.60	57.40

(a) **What will be the entries in the general ledger?**

Account name	Amount £	Debit ✓	Credit ✓
▼			
▼			
▼			
▼			
▼			

Picklist:

Other purchases
Polish/varnish purchases
Purchases ledger control
Purchases returns
Sales
Sales ledger control
Sales returns
Stationery
Wood purchases
VAT

(b) **What will be the entries in the purchases ledger?**

Account name		Amount £	Debit ✓	Credit ✓
	▼			
	▼			
	▼			
	▼			

Picklist:

Calverley Bros
Cavendish Woods
Culverden & Co
Ephraim Supplies
Discounts received
Other purchases
Polish/varnish purchases
Purchases day book
Purchases ledger control
Purchases returns
VAT
Wood purchases

Task 10.5

Shown below is Natural Productions' purchases returns day book.

Purchases returns day book

Date	Supplier	Credit note number	Total £	VAT £	Net £	Purchases £	Stationery £
10 Mar	K Mates	0326	235.20	39.20	196.00	196.00	
16 Mar	R Jones	C55	134.40	22.40	112.00		112.00
30 Mar	X & Y Ltd	563	297.60	49.60	248.00	248.00	
			667.20	111.20	556.00	444.00	112.00

(a) **What will be the entries in the general ledger?**

Account name		Amount £	Debit ✓	Credit ✓
	▼			
	▼			
	▼			
	▼			
	▼			

Picklist:

Packaging
Purchases
Purchases ledger control
Purchases returns
Sales
Sales ledger control
Sales returns
Stationery
VAT

(b) **What will be the entries in the purchases ledger?**

Account name	Amount £	Debit ✓	Credit ✓
▼			
▼			
▼			

Picklist:

K Mates
Purchases
Purchases ledger control
Purchases returns
R Jones
Sales
Sales ledger control
Sales returns
VAT
X & Y Ltd

Task 10.6

Shown below is Natural Productions' purchases returns day book.

Purchases returns day book

Date	Supplier	Credit note number	Total £	VAT £	Net £	Purchases £	Stationery £	Packaging £
10 Jan	P J Phillips	04216	117.60	19.60	98.00	98.00		
16 Jan	W J Jones	CN0643	67.20	11.20	56.00		56.00	
30 Jan	O & P Ltd	CN1102	148.80	24.80	124.00	124.00		
			333.60	55.60	278.00	222.00	56.00	

(a) **Post the totals of the purchases returns day book to the general ledger accounts given.**

General ledger

Purchases ledger control

Details		£	Details	£
	▼		Purchases	2,711.00
	▼		Stationery	314.00
	▼		Packaging	432.00
	▼		VAT	691.40
	▼		▼	
	▼		▼	

Picklist:

Packaging
Purchases
Purchases ledger control
Purchases returns
Sales
Sales ledger control
Sales returns
Stationery
VAT

VAT

Details	£	Details		£
Purchases ledger control	691.40		▼	
▼			▼	

Picklist:

Packaging
Purchases
Purchases ledger control
Purchases returns
Sales
Sales ledger control
Sales returns
Stationery
VAT

Purchases returns

Details		£	Details		£
	▼			▼	
	▼			▼	

Picklist:

Packaging
Purchases
Purchases ledger control
Purchases returns
Sales
Sales ledger control
Sales returns
Stationery
VAT

Stationery

Details		£	Details		£
Purchases ledger control		314.00		▼	
	▼			▼	

Picklist:

Packaging
Purchases
Purchases ledger control
Purchases returns
Sales
Sales ledger control
Sales returns
Stationery
VAT

(b) **Post the individual entries to the purchases ledger accounts also given below.**

Purchases ledger

P J Phillips

Details		£	Details		£
	▼		Purchases day book		428.40
	▼		Purchases day book		495.60
	▼			▼	

Picklist:

PJ Phillips
Purchases day book
Purchases returns day book
VAT

W J Jones

Details		£	Details		£
	▼		Purchases day book		252.00
	▼		Purchases day book		124.80
	▼			▼	

Picklist:

Purchases day book
Purchases returns day book
VAT
WJ Jones

O & P Ltd

Details		£	Details		£
	▼		Purchases day book		748.80
	▼			▼	

Picklist:

O & P Ltd
Purchases day book
Purchases returns day book
VAT

Task 10.7

You work for Natural Productions and one of your duties is to transfer data from the cash book to the ledgers. Most of the payments are to credit suppliers but there are some cash purchases of materials from small suppliers which include VAT. The cash book – credit side is shown below.

Cash book – credit side

Date	Details	Cash £	Bank £	VAT £	Cash purchases £	Trade payables £
23 Jan	Trenter Ltd		1,105.07			1,105.07
23 Jan	Cash purchase	108.00		18.00	90.00	
24 Jan	W J Jones		252.00			252.00
		108.00	1,357.07	18.00	90.00	1,357.07

(a) What will be the entries in the general ledger?

Account name	Amount £	Debit ✓	Credit ✓
▼			
▼			
▼			

Picklist:

Cash
Bank
Purchases
Purchases ledger control
Purchases returns
Sales
Sales ledger control
Sales returns
Trade payables
VAT

(b) What will be the entries in the purchases ledger?

Account name	Amount £	Debit ✓	Credit ✓
▼			
▼			

Picklist:

Purchases
Purchases ledger control
Purchases returns
Sales
Sales ledger control
Sales returns
Trenter Ltd
VAT
W J Jones

Task 10.8

The following credit transactions all took place on 30 November and have been entered into the purchases day book as shown below. No entries have yet been made in the ledgers.

Purchases day book

Date 20XX	Details	Invoice number	Total £	VAT @ 20% £	Net £
30 Nov	Frankie's Leatherware	0923	12,348	2,058	10,290
30 Nov	Casaubon's	C6478	3,924	654	3,270
	Totals		16,272	2,712	13,560

(a) **What will be the entries in the purchases ledger?**

Purchases ledger

Account name	Amount £	Debit ✓	Credit ✓
▼			
▼			

Picklist:

Casaubon's
Frankie's Leatherware
Purchases
Purchases ledger control
Purchases returns
Sales
Sales ledger control
Sales returns
VAT

(b) What will be the entries in the general ledger?

General ledger

Account name	Amount £	Debit ✓	Credit ✓
▼			
▼			
▼			

Picklist:

Casaubon's
Frankie's Leatherware
Purchases
Purchases ledger control
Purchases returns
Sales
Sales ledger control
Sales returns
VAT

. . . .

Task 10.9

Natural Productions' discounts received day book is shown below. No entries have yet been made into the ledgers.

Discounts received day book

Date 20XX	Customer	Credit note number	Total £	VAT £	Net £
3 May	Trenter Ltd	1501	36	6	30
10 May	WJ Jones	1502	72	12	60
			108	18	90

(a) **What will be the entries in the purchases ledger?**

Purchases ledger

Account name		Amount £	Debit ✓	Credit ✓
	▼			
	▼			

Picklist:

Discounts allowed
Discounts received
Purchases
Purchases ledger control
Purchases returns
Sales
Sales ledger control
Sales returns
Trenter Ltd
VAT
WJ Jones

(b) **What will be the entries in the general ledger?**

General ledger

Account name		Amount £	Debit ✓	Credit ✓
	▼			
	▼			
	▼			

Picklist:

Discounts allowed
Discounts received
Purchases
Purchases ledger control
Purchases returns
Sales
Sales ledger control
Sales returns
Trenter Ltd
VAT
WJ Jones

Task 10.10

The following transactions all took place on 30 November and have been entered in the credit side of the cash book as shown below. No entries have yet been made in the ledgers.

Cash book – Credit side

Date 20XX	Details	VAT @ 20% £	Bank £
30 Nov	Cash purchase	102	612
30 Nov	Casaubon's		2,445

(a) **What will be the entry in the purchases ledger?**

Purchases ledger

Account name	Amount £	Debit ✓	Credit ✓
▼			

Picklist:

Bank
Casaubon's
Discounts allowed
Discounts received
Purchases
Purchases ledger control
Sales
Sales ledger control
VAT

(b) **What will be the three entries in the general ledger?**

General ledger

Account name	Amount £	Debit ✓	Credit ✓
▼			
▼			
▼			

Picklist:

Bank
Casaubon's
Discounts allowed
Discounts received
Purchases
Purchases ledger control
Sales
Sales ledger control
VAT

Task 10.11

These are totals of the cash book at the end of the month.

Cash book

Cash £	Bank £	VAT £	Trade receivables £	Cash sales £	Cash £	Bank £	VAT £	Trade payables £	Cash purchases £
550	6,893	59	4,368	295	550	6,893	----	2,492	------

What will be the entries in the general ledger?

Account name		Amount £	Debit ✓	Credit ✓
	▼			
	▼			
	▼			
	▼			

Picklist:

Bank
Cash
Cash purchases
Cash sales
Purchases ledger control
Sales ledger control
VAT

Chapter 11 Accounting for petty cash

Task 11.1

Natural Productions has a petty cash system based on an imprest amount of £100 which is replenished weekly. On Friday 20 January the total of the vouchers in the petty cash box was £68.34.

How much cash is required to replenish the petty cash box?

£	

Task 11.2

Newmans, the music shop, has an imprest petty cash system based upon an imprest amount of £120.00. During the week ending 29 January the petty cash vouchers given below were presented, authorised and paid.

Petty cash voucher 0721	
	29 January 20XX
	£
Coffee	3.99
VAT is not applicable.	

Petty cash voucher 0722	
	29 January 20XX
	£
Taxi	8.94
VAT @ 20%	1.78
Total	10.72

(a) **Complete the petty cash book by:**

- **Entering both transactions into the petty cash book below.**

- **Totalling the petty cash book and inserting the balance carried down at 29 January.**

Petty cash book

Date 20XX	Details	Amount £	Date 20XX	Details	Amount £	VAT £	Travel £	Office expenses £
24 Jan	Balance b/f	120.00	27 Jan	Paper	7.12	1.18		5.94
			29 Jan	▼				
			29 Jan	▼				
			29 Jan	▼				
	Total			**Totals**				

Picklist:

Balance b/f
Balance c/d
Coffee
Office expenses
Taxi
Travel
VAT

(b) **What will be the amount of cash withdrawn from the bank to restore the imprest level of £120.00?**

£ [ ]

Task 11.3

On the first day of every month cash is drawn from the bank to restore the petty cash imprest level to £75.

A summary of petty cash transactions during November is shown below:

Opening balance on 1 November	£22
Cash from bank on 1 November	£53
Expenditure during month	£16

(a) **What will be the amount required to restore the imprest level on 1 December?**

£ [ ]

(b) **Will the receipt from the bank on 1 December be a debit or credit entry in the petty cash book?**

	✓
Debit	
Credit	

Task 11.4

Short Furniture has a monthly petty cash imprest system based upon an imprest amount of £150.00. During the month of January the following petty cash vouchers were authorised and paid:

Voucher No.	£
0473	12.60
0474	15.00
0475	19.75
0476	9.65
0477	10.00
0478	13.84
0479	4.26
0480	16.40

The cash in the petty cash box at 31 January was made up as follows:

£10 note	1
£5 note	4
£2 coin	3
£1 coin	7
50p coin	5
20p coin	8
10p coin	9
5p coin	4
2p coin	11
1p coin	8

(a) Add together the voucher total and the petty cash in the box to arrive at the imprest amount at the end of January.

	£
Voucher total	
Petty cash in the box	
Imprest amount	

(b) The petty cash control account in the general ledger is given below. You are to balance the petty cash control account (this should be the same as the balance of cash in the petty cash box on 31 January).

Petty cash control

		£			£
1 Jan	Balance b/f	150.00	31 Jan	Expenditure	101.50
▼		▼		▼	▼
	Total			Total	
▼		▼	▼		▼

Picklist:

31 Jan
1 Feb
Balance b/d
Balance c/d
Petty cash
VAT

....

Task 10.5

A business which is not registered for VAT has partially completed its petty cash book for November, as shown below.

(a) Complete the analysis columns for the four items purchased from petty cash.

(b) Total and balance the petty cash book, showing clearly the balance carried down at 30 November.

(c) Enter the balance brought down at 1 December, showing clearly the date, details, and amount. You do NOT need to restore the imprest amount.

Petty cash book

Debit side			Credit side					
Date	Details	Amount £	Date	Details	Total £	Stationery £	Postage £	Motor fuel £
1 Nov	Bal b/f	100	7 Nov	Postage stamps	20			
			15 Nov	Pens & pencils	18			
			22 Nov	Petrol	10			
			30 Nov	Envelopes	15			
▼	▼		▼	▼				
	Total			Total				
▼	▼		▼	▼				

Picklist:

30 Nov
1 Dec
Balance b/d
Balance c/d
Envelopes
Pens & pencils
Petrol
Postage stamps
VAT

Task 11.6

This is a summary of petty cash payments made by your business.

Post Office paid	£30.00 (no VAT)
Window cleaning paid	£25.60 plus VAT
MegaBus Company paid	£29.50 (no VAT)

(a) **Enter the above transactions in the petty cash book.**
(b) **Total the petty cash book and show the balance carried down.**

Petty cash book

Debit side		Credit side					
Details	Amount £	Details	Amount £	VAT £	Postage £	Travel £	Cleaning £
Bal b/f	175.00	▼					
		▼					
		▼					
▼		▼					
Total		Total					

Picklist:

Balance b/d
Balance c/d
Cleaning
MegaBus
Post Office
Postage
Travel
VAT
Window cleaning

Task 11.7

On 20 September the petty cash control account has a balance of £96.70. The cash in the petty cash box is checked and the following notes and coins are there.

Notes and coins	£
2 × £20 notes	40.00
3 × £10 notes	30.00
2 × £5 notes	10.00
1 × £2 coins	2.00
5 × £1 coins	5.00
7 × 50p coins	3.50
11 × 10p coins	1.10
2 × 5p coins	0.10

(a) **Reconcile the cash amount in the petty cash box with the balance on the petty cash control account.**

Amount in petty cash box	£	
Balance on petty cash control account	£	
Difference	£	

At the end of September the cash in the petty cash box was £9.76.

(b) **Complete the petty cash reimbursement document below to restore the imprest amount of £250.**

Petty cash reimbursement		
Date: 30.09.20XX		
Amount required to restore the cash in the petty cash box	£	

··

Task 11.8

This is a summary of petty cash payments made by Kitchen Kuts.

Tom's Taxi paid	£18.00 (no VAT)
Post Office paid	£30.00 (no VAT)
SMP Stationery paid	£36.00 plus VAT

(a) **Enter the above transactions, in the order in which they are shown, in the petty cash book below.**

(b) **Total the petty cash book and show the balance carried down.**

Petty cash book

Debit side		Credit side					
Details	Amount £	Details	Amount £	VAT £	Postage £	Travel £	Stationery £
Balance b/f	150.00	▼					
		▼					
		▼					
▼		▼					
Total		Total					

Picklist:
Balance b/f
Balance c/d
Post Office
Postage
SMP Stationery
Stationery
Tom's Taxi
Travel
VAT

Task 11.9

Part way through a month the petty cash control account had a balance of £120.00. The cash in the petty cash box was checked and the following notes and coins were there.

Notes and coins	£
3 × £20 notes	60.00
5 × £5 notes	25.00
17 × £1 coins	17.00
23 × 50p coins	11.50
16 × 10p coins	1.60
21 × 5p coins	1.05

(a) **Reconcile the cash amount in the petty cash box with the balance on the petty cash control account.**

Amount in petty cash box	£	
Balance on petty cash control account	£	
Difference	£	

At the end of the month the cash in the petty cash box was £3.45.

(b) **Complete the petty cash reimbursement document below to restore the imprest amount of £200.**

Petty cash reimbursement		
Date: 31.07.20XX		
Amount required to restore the cash in the petty cash box	£	

BPP
LEARNING MEDIA

Task 11.10

Ken trades in exotic dress materials. The following is the credit side of Ken's Petty Cash Book, which acts only as a book of prime entry.

Petty cash book – credit side

Details	Voucher number	Total £	VAT £	Office expenses £	Stationery £	Maintenance £
Tea, coffee and milk for office	1234	15.20		15.20		
Printer cartridge	1235	39.12	6.52		32.60	
Repair to fire extinguisher	1236	54.00	9.00			45.00
Totals		108.32	15.52	15.20	32.60	45.00

(a) **What will be the five entries in the general ledger?**

General ledger

Account name	Amount £	Debit ✓	Credit ✓
▼			
▼			
▼			
▼			
▼			

Picklist:
Bank
Cash
Maintenance
Office expenses
Petty cash
Purchases
Stationery
VAT

(b) **Which entry would be omitted if Ken's Petty Cash Book operated as a general ledger account as well?**

▼

Picklist:
Bank
Cash
Maintenance
Office expenses
Petty cash
Purchases
Stationery
VAT

Task 11.11

Benjamin operates a petty cash system whereby each week he withdraws £50 from the bank and puts it in the petty cash tin.

What type of system is this?

	✓
Imprest system	
Non-imprest system	

Task 11.12

Lucy operates a petty cash system whereby each Friday afternoon she puts £60 in to the petty cash tin. At the start of the week, Lucy had £75.23 in notes and coins in her petty cash tin.

This is a summary of petty cash payments made by Lucy during the week.

Taxi paid	£9.00 (no VAT)
Post Office paid	£15.00 (no VAT)
Suzie's Stationery paid	£36.00 plus VAT

On Friday afternoon, Lucy withdrew £60 from the bank and put it in the petty cash tin.

(a) **Enter the above transactions, in the order in which they are shown, in the petty cash book below.**

(b) **Total the petty cash book and show the balance carried down.**

Petty cash book

Debit side		Credit side						
Details	Amount £	Details	Amount £	VAT £	Postage £	Travel £	Stationery £
Balance b/f	75.23	▼					
		▼					
		▼					
▼		▼					
Total		Total					

Picklist:
Balance b/f
Balance c/d
Post Office
Postage
Stationery
Suzie's Stationery
Taxi
Travel
VAT

(c) **What is the balance in notes and coins in the petty cash tin on Friday after Lucy has added the £60 withdrawn from the bank?**

£	

··

Task 11.13

Sumberton Ltd maintains a petty cash-book as a book of prime entry and part of the double entry bookkeeping system. This is a summary of petty cash transactions in a week.

Stamps bought for £12.60, VAT not applicable.
Staplers bought for £18.90, including VAT.

(a) **Enter the above transactions into the partially completed petty cash-book below.**

(b) **Total the petty cash-book and show the balance carried down.**

Petty cash book

Details	Amount £	Details	Amount £	VAT £	Postage £	Stationery £
Balance b/f	175.00	Printer cartridges	17.40	2.90		14.50
Total		Totals				

Picklist:

Balance b/f
Balance c/d
Postage
Stamps
Staplers
Stationery
VAT

(c) **What will be the three accounts in the general ledger which will record the above transactions?**

General ledger accounts	
Stamps	
Stationery	
Petty cash-book	
Petty cash control	
Postage	
Staplers	
VAT	

(d) **Complete the following statement by choosing one word.**

In order to top up the petty cash to the imprest amount, the petty cashier needs to prepare a

Remittance advice note	
Cheque requisition form	
Petty cash claim	
Customer statement	

At the start of the next week cash was withdrawn from the bank to restore the imprest level of £175.

(e) What is the amount of cash that would have been withdrawn from the bank to restore the imprest level?

£ [   ]

These are the notes and coins that are now in the petty cash box.

Notes and coins
3 × £20 notes
2 x £10 notes
3 × £5 notes
14 × £1 coins
3 × 50p coins
3 × 20p coins

(f) Does the amount of cash in the petty cash box reconcile with the balance in the petty cash-book?

Yes, the amount of cash in the petty cash box reconciles with the balance in the petty cash-book	
No, there is not enough cash in the petty cash box	
No, there is too much cash in the petty cash box	

Chapter 12 Initial trial balance

Task 12.1

You are given the following account balances from the general ledger of your organisation.

Would each balance be a debit or a credit balance in the trial balance?

Ledger account	Balance	Debit ✓	Credit ✓
Sales	592,513		
Telephone	1,295		
Sales ledger control	52,375		
Wages	104,288		
Purchases returns	8,229		
Bank overdraft	17,339		
Purchases	372,589		
Drawings	71,604		
Sales returns	32,800		
Car	14,700		
Purchases ledger control	31,570		

Task 12.2

Below are two general ledger accounts and a partially completed trial balance at 31 January 20XX.

Complete the trial balance by:

- **Transferring the balances of the two general ledger accounts to the debit or credit column of the trial balance.**

- **Entering the amounts shown against each of the other account names into the debit or credit column of the trial balance.**

- **Totalling both columns of the trial balance**

Do not enter figures with decimal places in this task and do not enter a zero in unused column cells.

Office equipment

Date 20XX	Details	Amount £	Date 20XX	Details	Amount £
9 Jan	Balance b/f	29,502	1 Jan	Journal	350
31Jan	Bank	7,288	21 Jan	Balance c/d	36,440
		36,790			36,790

Purchases

Date 20XX	Details	Amount £	Date 20XX	Details	Amount £
1 Jan	Balance b/f	89,920	30 Jan	Balance c/d	196,800
30 Jan	Purchases ledger control	106,880			
		196,800			196,800

	£	Debit £	Credit £
Office equipment			
Purchases			
Motor vehicles	76,800		
Sales	285,600		
Bank (overdraft)	2,016		
Petty cash	36		
Capital	90,000		
Sales returns	5,640		
Purchases returns	4,320		
Sales ledger control	42,960		
Purchases ledger control	36,120		
VAT (owed to HMRC)	15,540		
Drawings	12,040		
Telephone	1,920		
Electricity	3,360		
Wages	74,520		
Loan from bank	36,000		

	£	Debit £	Credit £
Discounts allowed	7,680		
Discounts received	4,680		
Rent expense	16,080		
Totals			

Task 12.3

The double-entry system of bookkeeping normally results in which of the following balances on the ledger accounts? Tick ONE.

Debit balances	Credit balances	✓
Assets and income	Liabilities, capital and expenses	
Income, capital and liabilities	Assets and expenses	
Assets and expenses	Liabilities, capital and income	
Assets, expenses and capital	Liabilities and income	

Task 12.4

What does a credit balance on a ledger account indicates? Tick ONE.

	✓
An asset or an expense	
A liability or an expense	
An amount owing to the organisation	
A liability or income	

Task 12.5

Which of the following balances would be a credit balance on a trial balance?

	✓
Non-current assets	
Sales returns	
Discounts allowed	
Bank overdraft	

Task 12.6

Given below is the list of ledger balances for your organisation at 31 August.

You are required to prepare a trial balance as at 31 August.

	£	Debit £	Credit £
Bank (overdraft)	4,838		
Capital	216,000		
Discounts allowed	18,432		
Discounts received	11,232		
Drawings	28,896		
Electricity	8,064		
Loan from bank	86,400		
Motor vehicles	184,320		
Office equipment	87,456		
Petty cash	100		
Purchases	472,320		
Purchases ledger control	86,688		
Purchases returns	10,368		
Rent expense	38,592		
Sales	685,440		
Sales ledger control	103,104		
Sales returns	13,536		

	£	Debit £	Credit £
Telephone	4,608		
VAT (owed to HMRC)	37,310		
Wages	178,848		
Totals			

Answer Bank

Answer Bank

Bookkeeping Transactions Answer Bank

Chapter 1

Task 1.1

	Cash transaction ✓	Credit transaction ✓
Purchase of goods for £200 payable by cash in one week's time		✓
Writing a cheque for the purchase of a new computer	✓	
Sale of goods to a customer where the invoice accompanies the goods		✓
Receipt of a cheque from a customer for goods purchased today	✓	
Purchase of goods where payment is due in three weeks' time		✓

Task 1.2

The correct answer is: an invoice

Task 1.3

The correct answer is: a goods returned note

Task 1.4

(a)

	Document issued by Joe
Freddie asks Joe for a quote for 14 desks	Quotation
Joe delivers 14 desks to Freddie	Delivery note
Joe requests payment from Freddie	Invoice
Freddie pays his invoice and takes a prompt payment discount	Credit note

(b)

	Document issued by Freddie
Freddie places an order with Joe for 14 desks	Purchase order
Freddie accepts in to his warehouse delivery of 14 desks from Joe	Goods received note
Freddie returns one faulty desk to Joe	Goods returned note
Freddie pays his invoice	Remittance advice

Task 1.5

The correct answer is: an alpha-numeric system

Task 1.6

Customer	Customer code
Caledonian Ltd	Ca01
Jury's Brewery Ltd	Ju02

Task 1.7

The correct answer is: supplier code

Task 1.8

(a)

Supplier code	PL244
General ledger code	GL001

(b) The correct answer is: Product code

Task 1.9

(a)

Supplier account code	VIN234
General ledger code	GL505

(b) The correct answer is: to help trace relevant accounts quickly and easily

Chapter 2

Task 2.1

Date 20XX	Details	Invoice number	Total £	VAT £	Net £
7 August	VXT Ltd	172	120	20	100

Tutorial note. Working: VAT = 100 × 20%, Gross amount = 100 + 20 = 120

Task 2.2

Date 20XX	Details	Invoice number	Total £	VAT £	Net £
15 June	R Hart	365	648.00	108.00	540.00

Task 2.3

(a) – (b) Sales day book

Customer	Invoice number	Total £	VAT £	Net £
Hoppers Ltd	6237	656.40	109.40	547.00
Body Perfect	6238	744.00	124.00	620.00
Esporta Leisure	6239	415.20	69.20	346.00
Langans Beauty	6240	273.60	45.60	228.00
Body Perfect	6241	657.60	109.60	548.00
Superior Products	6242	265.20	44.20	221.00
Esporta Leisure	6243	499.20	83.20	416.00
Hoppers Ltd	6244	285.60	47.60	238.00
Langans Beauty	6245	328.80	54.80	274.00
		4,125.60	687.60	3,438.00

Cross-cast check:

	£
Net	3,438.00
VAT	687.60
Total	4,125.60

Task 2.4

Day book:	Sales returns day book

Customer	Credit note number	Total £	VAT £	Net £
Hoppers Ltd	1476	82.44	13.74	68.70
Esporta Leisure	1477	107.04	17.84	89.20
Superior Products	1478	14.10	2.35	11.75

Task 2.5

Day book:	Purchases day book

Date	Supplier	Invoice number	Total £	VAT £	Purchases (materials) £	Stationery £
4 Jan	P J Phillips	03576	428.40	71.40	357.00	
6 Jan	W J Jones	18435	252.00	42.00		210.00

Task 2.6

Day book:			Purchases day book				

Date	Supplier	Invoice number	Total £	VAT £	Purchases (materials) £	Stationery £	Packaging £
12 Jan	P J Phillips	03598	495.60	82.60	413.00		
16 Jan	Packing Supplies	28423	321.60	53.60			268.00
19 Jan	Trenter Ltd	18478	625.20	104.20	521.00		
20 Jan	O & P Ltd	84335	748.80	124.80	624.00		
24 Jan	Packing Supplies	28444	196.80	32.80			164.00
28 Jan	Trenter Ltd	18491	441.60	73.60	368.00		
31 Jan	W J Jones	43681	124.80	20.80		104.00	

Task 2.7

Day book:			Purchases returns day book				

Date	Supplier	Credit note number	Total £	VAT £	Purchases (materials) £	Stationery £	Packaging £
10 Jan	P J Phillips	04216	117.60	19.60	98.00		
16 Jan	W J Jones	CN 0643	67.20	11.20		56.00	

Task 2.8

Date	Customer	Credit note number	Customer code	Gross total £	VAT £	Net £
21 Sep	Whitehill Superstores	08650	SL 44	356.40	59.40	297.00
23 Sep	Dagwell Enterprises	08651	SL 15	244.80	40.80	204.00
	Totals			601.20	100.20	501.00

Task 2.9

Date	Supplier	Invoice number	Supplier code	Total £	VAT £	Net £	Wood purchases £	Polish/ varnish purchases £	Other purchases £
27 Jan	Ephraim Supplies	09642	PL39	349.20	58.20	291.00	291.00		
27 Jan	Cavendish Woods	06932	PL14	846.12	141.02	705.10	705.10		
27 Jan	Calverley Bros	67671	PL03	174.72	29.12	145.60		145.60	
27 Jan	Culverden & Co	36004	PL23	68.88	11.48	57.40			57.40
				1,438.92	239.82	1,199.10	996.10	145.60	57.40

Task 2.10

(a) – (b)

Sales returns day book

Date 20XX	Details	Credit note number	Total £	VAT @ 20% £	Net £	Bags returns £	Suitcases returns £
30 Nov	Shrier Goods	562	624	104	520	520	
30 Nov	Gringles Co	563	408	68	340		340
30 Nov	Lester plc	564	1,068	178	890	890	
	Totals		2,100	350	1,750	1,410	340

Chapter 3

Task 3.1

The correct answer is: a trade discount

Task 3.2

The correct answer is: HM Revenue & Customs

Task 3.3

Goods total	Trade discount (15% × price) £	Net total £
£416.80	62.52	354.28
£105.60	15.84	89.76
£96.40	14.46	81.94
£263.20	39.48	223.72
£351.00	52.65	298.35

Task 3.4

Net total	VAT (Net × 20%) £	Gross total £
£258.90	51.78	310.68
£316.80	63.36	380.16
£82.60	16.52	99.12
£152.70	30.54	183.24
£451.30	90.26	541.56

Task 3.5

Gross total £	VAT (Invoice total × 20/120) £	Net total £
145.20	24.20	121.00
66.90	11.15	55.75
246.60	41.10	205.50
35.40	5.90	29.50
125.40	20.90	104.50

Task 3.6

Invoice total £	VAT (Invoice total × 20/120) £	Net total £
252.66	42.11	210.55
169.20	28.20	141.00
48.60	8.10	40.50
104.28	17.38	86.90
60.48	10.08	50.40
822.60	137.10	685.50

Task 3.7

Customer	Gross invoice total £	Amount £
J Smith	258	250.26
Anchorage Ltd	312	302.64
VIP Ltd	84	81.48
Blue House Ltd	150	145.50

Tutorial note. Multiply the gross total by 97% to give the amount payable by each customer.

Task 3.8

	£
Net amount before discounts	7,000
Net amount after discounts	6,517
VAT	1,303.4
Total	7,820.4

Tutorial note.

Workings:

	£
Net amount before discounts	200 × 35.00 = 7,000
Net amount after discounts:	
Trade discount	7,000 × 5% = 350
After trade discount	6,650
Bulk discount	6,650 × 2% = 133
Net amount after trade and bulk discounts	6,517
VAT @ 20%	6,517 × 20% = 1,303.4
Total	7,820.4

Task 3.9

(a) | £ | 1,382.40 |

Tutorial note.

Working: 1,280 × 1.2 × 90% = 1,382.40

(b)

Amount	£
Net amount	128.00
VAT	25.60
Gross amount	153.60

Tutorial note.

Working: Discount: 1,280 × 1.2 × 10% = 153.60, VAT = 153.60/6 = 25.60, Net amount = 153.60 − 25.60 = 128.00

Task 3.10

Day book:	Discounts allowed day book

Date 20XX	Details	Credit note number	Total £	VAT £	Net £
15 Oct	Shipper Ltd	223	67.20	11.20	56.00

Tutorial note. The credit note should be recorded in Anchor Supplies Ltd's discounts allowed day book as it is a discount allowed to a customer.

The name of the customer (Shipper Ltd) should be recorded in the 'details' column.

Task 3.11

Day book:	Discounts received day book

Date 20XX	Details	Credit note number	Total £	VAT £	Net £
10 Nov	Rent a Van Ltd	11	123.60	20.60	103.00

Tutorial note. The credit note should be recorded in Pop Ice Cream Ltd's discounts received day book as it is a discount received from a supplier.

The name of the supplier (Rent a Van Ltd) should be recorded in the 'details' column.

Task 3.12

(a) The correct answer is: £2,304

Working: Gross amount = ((£2,000 × 20%) + £2,000) = £2,400

Amount after discount = £2,400 × 96% = £2,304

(b) The correct answer is: £2,400 (£2,000 + £400)

Task 3.13

The correct answer is: trade discount

Task 3.14

	True ✓	False ✓
The book of original entry for discounts allowed is the petty cash book		✓
Input tax is the VAT suffered on purchases	✓	
A goods received note is a primary document for recording in the accounting records		✓

Chapter 4

Task 4.1

The correct answer is: a price list

Task 4.2

The correct answer is: allocate one of two sales codes to each invoice and use this to write up the invoices in the analysed sales day book

Task 4.3

Southfield Electrical
Industrial Estate
Benham DR6 2FF

SALES INVOICE 57104

Date: 9 Jan 20XX

To: Whitehill Superstores   Customer account code: SL 44
        28 Whitehill Park
        Benham, DR6 5LM   Purchase order no: 32431

Quantity of units	Product code	Price each £	Total amount after trade discount £	VAT £	Total £
8	6260	300	2,160	432	2,592

Terms: 4% prompt payment discount for payment within 10 days

Workings:

	Calculation	£
Total list price	8 × 300	2,400
Trade discount	2,400 × 10%	240
Net amount	2,400 – 240	2,160
VAT	2,160 × 20%	432
Total	2,160 + 432	2,592

Task 4.4

```
                        Southfield Electrical
                        Industrial Estate
                        Benham DR6 2FF

                        SALES INVOICE 57105

Date: 19 May 20XX

To:    Harper & Sons                Customer account code: SL 26
       30 High Street
       Benham,  DR6 4ST             Purchase order no: 04367
```

Quantity of units	Product code	Price each £	Total amount after discounts £	VAT £	Total £
6	6370	260	1,407.9	281.58	1,689.48

Terms: 3% prompt payment discount for payment within 14 days

Workings:

	Calculation	£
Total list price	6 × 260	1,560
Trade discount	1,560 × 5%	78
Net	1,560 – 78	1,482
Bulk discount	1,482 × 5%	74.1
Net after discounts	1,482 – 74.1	1,407.9
VAT	1,407.9 × 20%	281.58
Total	1,407.9 + 281.58	1,689.48

Task 4.5

(a)

Questions	Yes ✓	No ✓
Has the correct amount of goods been delivered?		✓
Has the correct product been delivered?	✓	
Have the correct codes been used on the invoice?		✓
Has the correct discount been applied?		✓

Tutorial note.

The invoice is for 15 toasters (as ordered) whereas the delivery note shows that only 12 were delivered. The correct product has been delivered, but the wrong product code has been used on the invoice (9046 instead of 9406), the purchase order number on the invoice is also incorrect, it should be 32202.

The customer was entitled to a 5% trade discount which has not been applied to the invoice. Additionally the invoice should state that the customer has been offered a 3% prompt payment discount.

(b)

Net amount £	VAT amount £	Gross amount £
171.00	34.20	205.20

Tutorial note.

Workings:

	Calculation	£
Total list price	12 × 15	180.00
Trade discount	180 × 5%	9.00
Net	180 – 9	171.00
VAT	171 × 20%	34.20
Total	171.00 + 34.20	205.20

Task 4.6

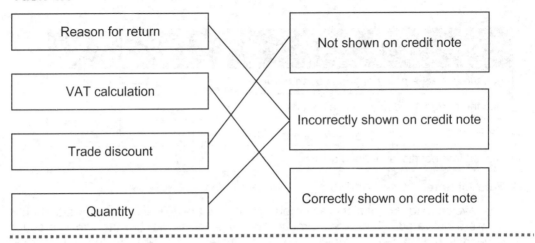

Task 4.7

(a)

Document names
Remittance advice note

(b)

> The cheque from Hayworth Ltd for £516.10 has resulted in an **underpayment**.
>
> This is because Hayworth has taken the **prompt payment discount** offered.
>
> This should not have been taken as the cheque arrived **13 days** after the invoice date.
>
> In order to resolve the problem Southfield Electrical should **request another cheque** from Hayworth Ltd for **£21.50** which will clear the outstanding balance.

Tutorial note.

Workings:

Prompt payment discount: £537.60 × 4% = £21.50 has been deducted: £537.60 − £21.50 = £516.10. This should not have been taken as the cheque arrived 13 days after the invoice date.

Task 4.8

> The cheque from Harper & Sons for £709.48 has resulted in an **underpayment**.
>
> Harper & Sons paid within the time limit for the **prompt payment discount** offered by Southfield Electrical.
>
> However, they **incorrectly calculated** the discount.
>
> In order to resolve the problem Southfield Electrical should **request another cheque** from Harper & Sons for **£4.76** which will clear the outstanding balance.

Tutorial note.

A discount of £34.52 (£744 – £709.48) has been taken, but it has been incorrectly calculated. The correct discount is £744 × 4% = £29.76. Therefore the cheque should have been made out for £34.52 – £29.76 = £4.76.

••

Task 4.9

Sumberton Ltd
Sumberton House,
10 Main Road
Sawlow
SA7 5LD

VAT Registration No. 536 3723 77

Gringles Co   Customer account code: SL637
Unit 18 Radley Estate
Sawlow
SA7 7VB

Date: 22 December 20XX

Invoice No: 12901
Delivery note number: 6734527

Quantity of goods	Product code	Total list price £	Net amount after bulk discount £	VAT £	Gross £
80	L736B	1,600	1,360	272	1,632

Tutorial note. Total list price: 80/5 × £100 = £1,600, Net amount after bulk discount = 1,600 × 85% = £1,360, VAT = 20% × £1,360 = £272, Gross = £1,360 + £272 = £1,632

Task 4.10

The correct answer is: Sales invoice 12813

··

Task 4.11

Sumberton Ltd
Sumberton House
10 Main Road
Sawlow
SA7 5LD

To: Diamond Bags   Date: 31 December 20XX

Date 20XX	Details	Transaction amount £	Outstanding amount £
10 December	Invoice 12905	1,902	1,902
12 December	Credit note 701	219	1,683
30 December	Invoice 12916	733	2,416
31 December	Cheque	1,668	748
31 December	Discount taken	15	733

··

Task 4.12

Ken's Exotics
1 Bath Street
Cembury, CE11 9SD

To: Crowley Ltd   Date: 31 October 20XX

Date 20XX	Details and Transaction amount £	Outstanding amount £
15 Sept	Invoice 1540 - £627	627
29 Sept	Invoice 1560 - £728	1,355
3 Oct	Credit note 89 - £46	1,309
10 Oct	Invoice 1580 - £1,209	2,518
15 Oct	Cheque - £581	1,937

··

Chapter 5

Task 5.1

When a supplier delivers materials to him he retains the supplier's delivery note and also prepares | **a goods received note** | once he has had a chance to inspect the quality of the items.

Task 5.2

The correct answer is: a product code

Task 5.3

(a) The correct answer is: 20 June

(b) The correct answer is: £281.30

   Workings:

   VAT: £239.20 × 20% = £47.84

   Invoice total: £239.20 + £47.84 = £287.04

   Discount: £287.04 × 2% = £5.74

   Payment: £287.04 − £5.74 = £281.30

Task 5.4

Invoice date	Supplier name	Payment date	Tutorial note. Workings	Amount of cheque £
5 Jan	Henson Press	27 Jan		336.00
8 Jan	GH Publications	3 Feb		136.80
12 Jan	Ely Instruments	27 Jan	765 × 98%	749.70
15 Jan	Hams Instruments	10 Feb		372.00
19 Jan	CD Supplies	10 Feb		138.72
22 Jan	Jester Press	27 Jan	156 × 96.5%	150.54
22 Jan	Henson Press	17 Feb		306.00

Task 5.5

(a)

Remittance advice		
To: PT Supplies Designs		**From: Edgehill**
Date: 7 February 20XX		

Date 20XX	Details and transaction amount £
6 Jan	Inv 20671 - £107
8 Jan	Inv 20692 - £157
10 Jan	CN 04722 - £28

(b)

£	236

Tutorial note. Working: £107 + £157 – £28 = £236

Task 5.6

(a)

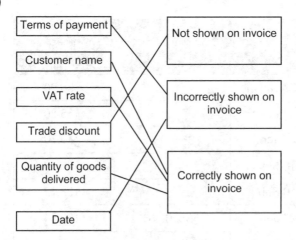

(b)

Net amount £	VAT amount £	Gross amount £
216.00	43.20	259.20

Tutorial note.

Working:

	Calculation	£
Net before discount	10 × 24	240
Trade discount	240 × 10%	24
Net amount	240 – 24	216
VAT	216 × 20%	43.20
Total	216 + 43.2	259.20

Task 5.7

(a)

	Yes ✓	No ✓
Has the correct purchase price of the rocking chairs been charged?	✓	
Has the correct discount been applied?		✓
Has the invoice been correctly cast?		✓
Has the correct product code been used on the invoice?		✓
Has VAT been charged at the correct rate?	✓	

Tutorial note.

- Trade discount of 5% instead of 10% agreed has been deducted.

- The invoice has been incorrectly cast – the total of the net and VAT amounts should be £1,751.04.

- The product code on the invoice does not agree to that on the purchase order.

(b)

Net amount £	VAT amount £	Gross amount £
1,382.40	276.48	1,658.88

Tutorial note.

Working:

	Calculation	£
Net before discount	16 × 96.00	1,536.00
Trade discount	1,536.00 × 10%	153.60
Net amount	1,536.00 – 153.60	1,382.40
VAT	1,382.40 × 20%	276.48
Total	1,382.40 + 276.48	1,658.88

Task 5.8

(a) The correct answer is: discount received £20

(b) The correct answer is: credit note 3215 £250

(c) The correct answer is: £723

Working:

£743 – £20 = £723

Task 5.9

	Yes ✓	No ✓
Has the correct purchase price of the cardboard boxes been charged?		✓
Has the correct discount been applied?		✓
What would be the VAT amount charged if the invoice was correct?	£	108.00
What would be the total amount charged if the invoice was correct?	£	648.00

Tutorial note.

Working:

	Calculation	£
Net before discount	30 × 20	600
Trade discount	600 × 10%	60
Net amount	600 – 60	540
VAT	540 × 20%	108
Total	540 + 108	648

Task 5.10

(a)

Ken's Exotics
1 Bath Street
Cembury, CE11 9SD
REMITTANCE ADVICE

To: Mack Materials   Date: 30 June 20XX

Please find attached our cheque in payment of the following amounts.

Invoice number	Credit note number	Amount £
Invoice 901		760
	Credit note 43	31
Total amount paid		729

(b) The correct answer is: the remittance advice note will be sent to the supplier to advise them of the amount being paid

Task 5.11

The correct answer is: Ken sent a cheque for £1,586 to the supplier on 30 June 20XX

Task 5.12

	Yes ✓	No ✓
Has the correct purchase price of the cabin cases been charged?		✓
Has the correct discount been applied?		✓
What would be the VAT amount charged if the invoice was correct?	£	58.65
What would be the total amount charged if the invoice was correct?	£	351.90

Tutorial note.

Workings:

VAT: (15 × £23) × 0.85 × 0.2 = £58.65

Total: (15 × £23 × 0.85) + £58.65 = £351.90

....

Task 5.13

(a) The correct answer is: discount of £10

(b) The correct answer is: credit note C579

(c) The correct answer is: £6,141

   Working:

   (£6,151 – £10)

(d) The correct answer is: an invoice adds to the amount owed to the supplier

....

Chapter 6

Task 6.1

	Asset ✓	Liability ✓
A trade receivable	✓	
A car used in the business	✓	
A loan from the bank		✓
A bank overdraft		✓
Cash in hand	✓	
VAT owed to HMRC		✓
A trade payable		✓
Inventory of raw materials	✓	

Task 6.2

An increase in an expense is a | debit |

A decrease in a liability is a | debit |

An increase in income is a | credit |

An increase in an asset is a | debit |

An increase in capital is a | credit |

A decrease in an asset is a | credit |

An increase in a liability is a | credit |

A decrease in capital is a | debit |

Task 6.3

(a) (i) James paid £20,000 into a business bank account in order to start the business.

Effect 1	Effect 2
Increase in cash	Increase in capital

(ii) He paid an initial rental of £2,500 by cheque for the shop that he is to trade from.

Effect 1	Effect 2
Decrease in cash	Rent expense incurred

(iii) He purchased a van by cheque for £7,400.

Effect 1	Effect 2
Decrease in cash	Increase in assets

(iv) He purchased £6,000 of goods for resale on credit.

Effect 1	Effect 2
Increase in purchases	Increase in liabilities (trade payables)

(v) He sold goods for £1,000 - the customer paid by cheque.

Effect 1	Effect 2
Increase in cash	Increase in sales

(vi) He sold goods on credit for £4,800.

Effect 1	Effect 2
Increase in assets (trade receivables)	Increase in sales

(vii) He paid shop assistants' wages by cheque totalling £2,100.

Effect 1	Effect 2
Decrease in cash	Wages expense incurred

(viii) He made further sales on credit for £3,900.

Effect 1	Effect 2
Increase in assets (trade receivables)	Increase in sales

(ix) He purchased a further £1,400 of goods for resale by cheque.

Effect 1	Effect 2
Decrease in cash	Increase in purchases

(x) £3,700 was received from credit customers.

Effect 1	Effect 2
Increase in cash	Decrease in assets (trade receivables)

(xi) He paid £3,300 to credit suppliers.

Effect 1	Effect 2
Decrease in cash	Decrease in liabilities (trade payables)

(xii) He withdrew £800 from the business for his living expenses.

Effect 1	Effect 2
Decrease in cash	Increase in drawings

(b)

Bank

Details	£	Details	£
Capital (i)	20,000	Rent (ii)	2,500
Sales (v)	1,000	Van (iii)	7,400
Sales ledger control (x)	3,700	Wages (vii)	2,100
		Purchases (ix)	1,400
		Purchases ledger control (xi)	3,300
		Drawings (xii)	800

Capital

Details	£	Details	£
		Bank (i)	20,000

Rent

Details	£	Details	£
Bank (ii)	2,500		

Van

Details	£	Details	£
Bank (iii)	7,400		

Purchases

Details	£	Details	£
Purchases ledger control (iv)	6,000		
Bank (ix)	1,400		

Purchases ledger control

Details	£	Details	£
Bank (xi)	3,300	Purchases (iv)	6,000

Sales account

Details	£	Details	£
		Bank (v)	1,000
		Sales ledger control (vi)	4,800
		Sales ledger control (viii)	3,900

Sales ledger control

Details	£	Details	£
Sales (vi)	4,800	Bank (x)	3,700
Sales (viii)	3,900		

Wages

Details	£	Details	£
Bank (vii)	2,100		

Drawings

Details	£	Details	£
Bank (xii)	800		

Task 6.4

(a)

	Debit ✓	Credit ✓
Discounts allowed	✓	
Sales ledger control		✓

(b)

	Debit ✓	Credit ✓
Discounts received		✓
Purchases ledger control	✓	

(c)

	Debit ✓	Credit ✓
Purchases	✓	
Purchases ledger control		✓

(d)

	Debit ✓	Credit ✓
Sales		✓
Sales ledger control	✓	

(e)

	Debit ✓	Credit ✓
Cash	✓	
Sales		✓

(f)

	Debit ✓	Credit ✓
Cash	✓	
Sales ledger control		✓

(g)

	Debit ✓	Credit ✓
Drawings	✓	
Cash		✓

(h)

	Debit ✓	Credit ✓
Wages	✓	
Cash		✓

Chapter 7

Task 7.1

TN Designs

Date 20XX	Details	Amount £	Date 20XX	Details	Amount £
1 May	Balance b/f	2,643	8 May	Bank	1,473
11 May	Invoice 27491	1,804	24 May	Credit note 381	265
18 May	Invoice 27513	1,088			
			31 May	Balance c/d	3,797
	Total	5,535		Total	5,535
1 Jun	Balance b/d	3,797			

Task 7.2

Harold & Partners

Date 20XX	Details	Amount £	Date 20XX	Details	Amount £
7 Sept	Bank	635	1 Sept	Balance b/f	1,367
7 Sept	Discount	33	5 Sept	Invoice 27465	998
30 Sept	Credit note 364	106	12 Sept	Invoice 27499	478
30 Sept	Balance c/d	2,069			
	Total	2,843		Total	2,843
			1 Oct	Balance b/d	2,069

Task 7.3

Account name	Debit £	Credit £
Purchases ledger control	379.98	
Bank		367.48
Discount received		12.50

Task 7.4

	Capital ✓	Revenue ✓
Purchase of a new computer paid for by cheque	✓	
Purchase of printer paper by cheque		✓
Purchase of a new business car on credit	✓	
Payment of road tax on a new business car		✓
Payment of rent for the business premises		✓

Task 7.5

Purchases ledger control

Date	Details	£	Date	Details	£
31 Oct	Purchases returns	4,467	1 Oct	Balance b/d	41,204
31 Oct	Bank	36,409	31 Oct	Purchases	52,390
31 Oct	Discounts received	125			
31 Oct	Balance c/d	52,593			
	Total	93,594		Total	93,594
			1 Nov	Balance b/d	52,593

Petty cash

Date	Details	£	Date	Details	£
1 Oct	Balance b/d	200.00	31 Oct	Expenses	183.25
31 Oct	Bank	183.25	31 Oct	Balance c/d	200.00
	Total	383.25		Total	383.25
1 Nov	Balance b/d	200.00			

VAT

Date	Details	£	Date	Details	£
31 Oct	Sales returns	40.00	1 Oct	Balance b/d	183.25
31 Oct	Purchases	1,900.00	31 Oct	Purchases returns	62.00
31 Oct	Balance c/d	1,555.25	31 Oct	Sales	3,250.00
	Total	3,495.25		Total	3,495.25
			1 Nov	Balance b/d	1,555.25

Task 7.6

	Capital ✓	Revenue ✓
Payment of a credit supplier for goods received for resale		✓
Receipt of proceeds from sale of car used in the business	✓	
Payment of drawings to the business owner	✓	
Acquisition of new machine for use over five years	✓	
Payment by a cash customer for goods		✓

Task 7.7

(a) – (c)

Purchases

Date 20XX	Details	Amount £	Date 20XX	Details	Amount £
01 Nov	Balance b/d	140,389			
15 Nov	Purchases ledger control	14,388			
30 Nov	Purchases ledger control	52,389			
			30 Nov	Balance c/d	207,166
	Total	207,166		Total	207,166
1 Dec	Balance b/d	207,166			

Bank interest received

Date 20XX	Details	Amount £	Date 20XX	Details	Amount £
			01 Nov	Balance b/d	32
			15 Nov	Bank	14
			30 Nov	Bank	22
30 Nov	Balance c/d	68			
	Total	68		Total	68
			1 Dec	Balance b/d	68

Task 7.8

Item	Capital expenditure ✓	Revenue expenditure ✓	Capital income ✓	Revenue income ✓
Payment in advance for 3 months of phone line rental		✓		
Proceeds from sale of machinery			✓	
Sale of suitcases for cash				✓
Receipt of payment from trade receivable for bags				✓
Purchase of a shop building	✓			
Petty cash payment for stationery		✓		

Task 7.9

Item	Example
Asset	Trade receivables
Liability	Bank overdraft
Capital transaction	Drawings

Chapter 8

Task 8.1

(a)

Details	Cash £	Bank £	VAT £	Cash purchases £	Trade payables £
Balance b/f		735			
Mendip plc	138		23	115	
W J Jones		521			521
Trenter Ltd		358			358
Packing Supplies		754			754
Total	138	2,368	23	115	1,633

(b) Cash balance is £381

Working: £200 + £319 − £138

(c) **Bank balance is** − £1,808

Working: £560 − £2,368

(d)

	✓
Debit	
Credit	✓

Task 8.2

Cash book – credit side

Details	Cash £	Bank £	VAT £	Trade payables £	Cash purchases £	Rent & rates £
Henson Press		329		329		
Ely Instruments		736		736		
Rates		255				255
Rent		500				500
Total		1,820		1,065		755

Task 8.3

Cash book – debit side

Details	Cash £	Bank £	VAT £	Trade receivables £	Cash sales £
Balance b/f	120	1,520			
Hoppers Ltd	334	500	139		695
Body Perfect		542		542	
Totals	454	2,562	139	542	695

Task 8.4

Cash book – debit side

Details	Cash £	Bank £	VAT £	Trade receivables £	Cash sales £
Balance b/f	56	1,805			
Howsham Ltd	210		35		175
Esporta Leisure		958		958	
Totals	266	2,763	35	958	175

Task 8.5

(a) Cash book – credit side

Details	Cash £	Bank £	VAT £	Trade payables £	Cash purchases £	Stationery £
Balance b/f		236				
Dubai Dreams	324		54		270	
Walter Enterprises	228		38		190	
Sinead Reilly	56				56	
Sumatra Trading		7,265		7,265		
SHSK Co		378	63			315
Total	608	7,879	155	7,265	516	315

(b) Cash book – debit side

Details	Cash £	Bank £	VAT £	Trade receivables £
Balance b/f	1,228			
Park Farm Stores		2,576		2,576
Tristram Pale Ltd		4,233		4,233
Total	1,228	6,809		6,809

(c) The correct answer is: £620

Working:

(1,228 – 608)

(d) The correct answer is: £1,070

Working:

(7,879 – 6,809)

(e) The correct answer is: Credit

Task 8.6

(a) **Cash book – credit side**

Details	Cash £	Bank £	VAT £	Trade payables £	Cash purchases £	Motor expenses £
Balance b/f		16,942				
B Smithson Ltd	240		40		200	
H Hamnet	192		32		160	
Renee Reid	320				320	
Tenon Ltd		3,600		3,600		
Vernon Motor Repairs		48	8			40
Total	752	20,590	80	3,600	680	40

(b) **Cash book – debit side**

Details	Cash £	Bank £	VAT £	Trade receivables £
Balance b/f	1,325			
G Brownlow		749		749
S Barnett		300		300
Total	1,325	1,049		1,049

(c) The correct answer is: £573

Working:

(1,325 – 752 = 573)

(d) The correct answer is: £19,541

Working:

(20,590 – 1,049 = 19,541)

(e) The correct answer is: Credit

Task 8.7

Cash book – debit side

Details	Cash £	Bank £	VAT £	Trade receivables £	Cash sales £
Balance b/f	55	1,300			
Whippet's	210		35		175
Ragdoll Ltd		958		958	
Totals	265	2,258	35	958	175
Balance b/d	265	1,165			

Cash book – credit side

Details	Cash £	Bank £	VAT £	Trade payables £	Cash purchases £
Hornsea Ltd		355		355	
Lyndon Plc		738		738	
Balance c/d	265	1,165			
Total	265	2,258		1,093	

Task 8.8

(a) **Cash book – debit side**

Details	Cash £	Bank £	VAT £	Trade receivables £	Cash sales £
Balance b/f	159	844			
Humber & Co	582		97		485
Ridgely Ltd		2,150		2,150	
Watts Partners		978		978	
Total	741	3,972	97	3,128	485

(b) The correct answer is: £ 180 (£741 – £561)

(c) The correct answer is: £ –113 (£3,972 – £4,085)

Chapter 9

Task 9.1

(a) Sales ledger

Account name	Amount £	Debit ✓	Credit ✓
S Himms	900	✓	
G Pood	1,500	✓	
M Kitchell	456	✓	
B Crown	1,392	✓	

(b) General ledger

Account name	Amount £	Debit ✓	Credit ✓
Sales	3,540		✓
VAT	708		✓
Sales ledger control	4,248	✓	

Task 9.2

(a) General ledger

Sales ledger control

Details	£	Details	£
Sales	7,085.00		
VAT	1,417.00		

Sales

Details	£	Details	£
		Sales ledger control	7,085.00

VAT

Details	£	Details	£
		Sales ledger control	1,417.00

(b) **Sales ledger**

H Simms SL 45

Details	£	Details	£
Sales day book	1,800.00		

K Mitchell SL 30

Details	£	Details	£
Sales day book	912.00		

Task 9.3

(a) **Sales ledger**

Account name	Amount £	Debit ✓	Credit ✓
Hoppers Ltd	656.40	✓	
Body Perfect	744.00	✓	

(b) **General ledger**

Account name	Amount £	Debit ✓	Credit ✓
Sales	1,167.00		✓
VAT	233.40		✓
Sales ledger control	1,400.40	✓	

Task 9.4

(a) **General ledger**

Sales ledger control

Details	£	Details	£
Sales	574.00		
VAT	114.80		

Sales

Details	£	Details	£
		Sales ledger control	574.00

VAT

Details	£	Details	£
		Sales ledger control	114.80

(b)   **Sales ledger**

Langans Beauty

Details	£	Details	£
Sales day book	273.60		

Esporta Leisure

Details	£	Details	£
Sales day book	415.20		

Task 9.5

(a) **Sales ledger**

Account name	Amount £	Debit ✓	Credit ✓
Rocks Garden Suppliers	701.76	✓	
Eridge Nurseries	429.30	✓	
Abergaven GC	923.40	✓	
Rother Nurseries	756.00	✓	

(b) **General ledger**

Account name	Amount £	Debit ✓	Credit ✓
Sales	2,342.05		✓
VAT	468.41		✓
Sales ledger control	2,810.46	✓	

Task 9.6

(a) Sales ledger

Account name	Amount £	Debit ✓	Credit ✓
Hoppers Ltd	82.44		✓
Esporta Leisure	107.04		✓
Superior Products	14.16		✓

(b) General ledger

Account name	Amount £	Debit ✓	Credit ✓
Sales returns	169.70	✓	
VAT	33.94	✓	
Sales ledger control	203.64		✓

Task 9.7

(a)

Account name	Amount £	Debit ✓	Credit ✓
Hoppers Ltd	36		✓
Esporta Leisure	72		✓

(b)

Account name	Amount £	Debit ✓	Credit ✓
Discounts allowed	90	✓	
VAT	18	✓	
Sales ledger control	108		✓

Task 9.8

(a)

	True ✓	False ✓
Rother Nurseries has fully settled their account at 31 January 20XX.		✓
Invoice 08695 should have been included in the payment in order to fully settle the account at 31 January.		✓
The remittance advice has been correctly cast.	✓	
The invoice amounts are included correctly on the remittance advice note.		✓

Tutorial note. Rother Nurseries has not fully settled its account as at 31 January because it has made a mistake in the amount included for invoice 08674. It has included this invoice as £114.78 instead of £214.78, therefore it still owes £100. Invoice 08695 is dated 5 February, so did not form part of the account as at 31 January and was correctly excluded from the payment.

(b)

£	1,212.17

Tutorial note. £756.00 + £214.78 + £378.89 – £96.50 = £1,212.17

··

Task 9.9

(a)

	True ✓	False ✓
Abergaven Garden Centre has included on the remittance advice note all relevant transactions up to 9 February.		✓
The remittance advice note has been correctly cast.		✓
The invoice amounts are included correctly on the remittance advice note.	✓	

Tutorial note. Abergaven Garden Centre has not included its credit notes with its payment. Therefore it has paid too much. The remittance advice has not been correctly cast as the final invoice has been excluded from the casting.

(b)

£	2,136.57

Tutorial note. 923.40 + 623.56 + 316.58 + 415.76 – 32.50 – 110.23 = £2,136.57

··

Task 9.10

Account name	Amount £	Debit ✓	Credit ✓
VAT	46.64		✓
Cash sales	233.20		✓
Sales ledger control	2,018.10		✓

Task 9.11

(a) Sales ledger

Hoppers Ltd

Details	£	Details	£
Invoice 6237	656.40	Credit note 1476	82.44
		Bank	553.96

Body Perfect

Details	£		£
Invoice 6238	744.00	Bank	706.64

Esporta Leisure

Details	£	Details	£
Invoice 6239	415.20	Credit note 1477	107.04
		Bank	367.20

Langans Beauty

Details	£	Details	£
Invoice 6240	273.60	Bank	273.60

Superior Products

Details	£	Details	£
Invoice 6242	265.20	Credit note 1478	14.16
		Bank	116.70

(b) General ledger

Cash

Details	£	Details	£
Sales	233.20		
VAT	46.64		

Bank

Details	£	Details	£
Sales ledger control	2,018.10		

Sales ledger control

Details	£	Details	£
Sales	3,438.00	Sales returns	169.70
VAT	687.60	VAT	33.94
		Bank	2,018.10

Sales

Details	£	Details	£
		Sales ledger control	3,438.00
		Cash	233.20

VAT

Details	£	Details	£
Sales ledger control	33.94	Sales ledger control	687.60
		Cash	46.64

Task 9.12

(a) Sales ledger

Account name	Amount £	Debit ✓	Credit ✓
Henderson & Co	7,349		✓

(b) General ledger

Account name	Amount £	Debit ✓	Credit ✓
Sales ledger control	7,349		✓
Sales	355		✓
VAT	71		✓

Task 9.13

(a) Sales ledger

Alpha Services			SL 10
Details	£	Details	£
Balance b/d	253.63	Credit note 551	624.00
Invoice 715	5,190.00	Bank	253.63
Invoice 787	10,020.00		

(b)

STATEMENT OF ACCOUNT

Southfield Electrical

Industrial Estate

Benham DR6 2FF

To: Alpha Services   Date: 31 May 20XX

Date and details	Transaction amount £	Outstanding amount £
1 May – Balance b/f		253.63
2 May – Payment received	253.63	0.00
7 May – Invoice 715	5,190.00	5,190.00
12 May – Credit note 551	624.00	4,566.00
17 May – Invoice 787	10,020.00	14,586.00

Task 9.14

(a) Sales ledger

Account name	Amount £	Debit ✓	Credit ✓
Gringles Co	300	✓	
Lester plc	1,308	✓	
Shrier Goods	2,676	✓	
Abunda Bags	1,992	✓	

(b) General ledger

Account name	Amount £	Debit ✓	Credit ✓
Sales ledger control	6,276	✓	
Sales	5,230		✓
VAT	1,046		✓

Chapter 10

Task 10.1

(a) Purchases day book

Date 20XX	Details	Invoice number	Total £	VAT £	Net £
30 June	Seashell Ltd	8971	3,853.20	642.20	3,211.00
30 June	Opal & Co	05119	4,800.00	800.00	4,000.00
	Totals		8,653.20	1,422.20	7,211.00

Tutorial note.

Workings:

Seashell Ltd VAT = 3,211 × 20% = 642.20, Gross = 3,211 + 642.20 = 3,853.20
Opal & Co VAT = 4,800/6 = 800, Net = 4,800 - 800 = 4,000

(b) Purchases ledger

Account name	Amount £	Debit ✓	Credit ✓
Seashell Ltd	3,853.20		✓
Opal & Co	4,800.00		✓

Task 10.2

(a)

Account name	Amount £	Debit ✓	Credit ✓
Purchases	2,711.00	✓	
Stationery	314.00	✓	
Packaging	432.00	✓	
VAT	691.40	✓	
Purchases ledger control	4,148.40		✓

(b)

Account name	Amount £	Debit ✓	Credit ✓
W J Jones	252		✓

Tutorial note.
Working: £210 × 20 % = £42, gross = £210 + £42 = £252

Task 10.3

(a) General ledger

Purchases ledger control

Details	£	Details	£
		Purchases	357.00
		Packaging	268.00
		VAT	125.00

VAT

Details	£	Details	£
Purchases ledger control	125.00		

Purchases

Details	£	Details	£
Purchases ledger control	357.00		

Packaging

Details	£	Details	£
Purchases ledger control	268.00		

(b) Purchases ledger

P J Phillips

Details	£	Details	£
		Purchases day book	428.40

Packing Supplies

Details	£	Details	£
		Purchases day book	321.60

Task 10.4

(a)

Account name	Amount £	Debit ✓	Credit ✓
Wood purchases	996.10	✓	
Polish/varnish purchases	145.60	✓	
Other purchases	57.40	✓	
VAT	239.82	✓	
Purchases ledger control	1,438.92		✓

(b)

Account name	Amount £	Debit ✓	Credit ✓
Calverley Bros	174.72		✓
Cavendish Woods	846.12		✓
Culverden & Co	68.88		✓
Ephraim Supplies	349.20		✓

Task 10.5

(a)

Account name	Amount £	Debit ✓	Credit ✓
Purchases returns	444.00		✓
Stationery	112.00		✓
VAT	111.20		✓
Purchases ledger control	667.20	✓	

(b)

Account name	Amount £	Debit ✓	Credit ✓
K Mates	235.20	✓	
R Jones	134.40	✓	
X & Y Ltd	297.60	✓	

....

Task 10.6

(a) General ledger

Purchases ledger control

Details	£	Details	£
Purchases returns	222.00	Purchases	2,711.00
Stationery	56.00	Stationery	314.00
VAT	55.60	Packaging	432.00
		VAT	691.40

VAT

Details	£	Details	£
Purchases ledger control	691.40	Purchases ledger control	55.60

Purchases returns

Details	£	Details	£
		Purchases ledger control	222.00

Stationery

Details	£	Details	£
Purchases ledger control	314.00	Purchases ledger control	56.00

(b) **Purchases ledger**

P J Phillips

Details	£	Details	£
Purchases returns day book	117.60	Purchases day book	428.40
		Purchases day book	495.60

W J Jones

Details	£	Details	£
Purchases returns day book	67.20	Purchases day book	252.00
		Purchases day book	124.80

O & P Ltd

Details	£	Details	£
Purchases returns day book	148.80	Purchases day book	748.80

Task 10.7

(a)

Account name	Amount £	Debit ✓	Credit ✓
Purchases	90.00	✓	
VAT	18.00	✓	
Purchases ledger control	1,357.07	✓	

(b)

Account name	Amount £	Debit ✓	Credit ✓
Trenter Ltd	1,105.07	✓	
W J Jones	252.00	✓	

Task 10.8

(a) **Purchases ledger**

Account name	Amount £	Debit ✓	Credit ✓
Frankie's Leatherware	12,348		✓
Casaubon's	3,924		✓

(b) **General ledger**

Account name	Amount £	Debit ✓	Credit ✓
Purchases ledger control	16,272		✓
Purchases	13,560	✓	
VAT	2,712	✓	

Task 10.9

(a) Purchases ledger

Account name	Amount £	Debit ✓	Credit ✓
Trenter Ltd	36	✓	
WJ Jones	72	✓	

(b) General ledger

Account name	Amount £	Debit ✓	Credit ✓
Discounts received	90		✓
VAT	18		✓
Purchases ledger control	108	✓	

Task 10.10

(a) Purchases ledger

Account name	Amount £	Debit ✓	Credit ✓
Casaubon's	2,445	✓	

(b) General ledger

Account name	Amount £	Debit ✓	Credit ✓
Purchases ledger control	2,445	✓	
Purchases	510	✓	
VAT	102	✓	

Task 10.11

What will be the entries in the general ledger?

Account name	Amount £	Debit ✓	Credit ✓
Sales ledger control	4,368		✓
Cash sales	295		✓
VAT	59		✓
Purchases ledger control	2,492	✓	

Chapter 11

Task 11.1

The correct answer is: £68.34

Task 11.2

(a) Petty cash book

Date 20XX	Details	Amount £	Date 20XX	Details	Amount £	VAT £	Travel £	Office expenses £
24 Jan	Balance b/f	120.00	27 Jan	Paper	7.12	1.18		5.94
			29 Jan	Coffee	3.99			3.99
			29 Jan	Taxi	10.72	1.78	8.94	
			29 Jan	Balance c/d	98.17			
	Total	120.00		**Totals**	120.00	2.96	8.94	9.93

(b) £ 21.83

Tutorial note. Working: £120 − £98.17 = £21.83

Task 11.3

(a) The correct answer is: £16

Working

	£
Opening balance	22
Cash from bank	53
Less: expenditure during month	(16)
balance at end of month	59

Therefore 75 − 59 = £16 required to restore the imprest level

(b) The correct answer is: Debit

Task 11.4

(a)

	Voucher total
	£
0473	12.60
0474	15.00
0475	19.75
0476	9.65
0477	10.00
0478	13.84
0479	4.26
0480	16.40
	101.50

Petty cash box		£
£10 note	1	10.00
£5 note	4	20.00
£2 coin	3	6.00
£1 coin	7	7.00
50p coin	5	2.50
20p coin	8	1.60
10p coin	9	0.90
5p coin	4	0.20
2p coin	11	0.22
1p coin	8	0.08
		48.50

	£
Voucher total	101.50
Petty cash in the box	48.50
Imprest amount	150.00

(b) Petty cash control

		£			£
1 Jan	Balance b/f	150.00	31 Jan	Expenditure	101.50
			31 Jan	Balance c/d	48.50
	Total	150.00		Total	150.00
1 Feb	Balance b/d	48.50			

Task 11.5

(a) – (c)

Date	Details	Amount £	Date	Details	Total £	Stationery £	Postage £	Motor fuel £
1 Nov	Bal b/f	100	7 Nov	Postage stamps	20		20	
			15 Nov	Pens and pencils	18	18		
			22 Nov	Petrol	10			10
			30 Nov	Envelopes	15	15		
					63			
			30 Nov	Bal c/d	37			
	Total	100		Total	100	33	20	10
1 Dec	Bal b/d	37						

Task 11.6

(a) – (b)

Petty cash book

Debit side		Credit side					
Details	Amount £	Details	Amount £	VAT £	Postage £	Travel £	Cleaning £
Bal b/f	175.00	Post Office	30.00		30.00		
		Window cleaning	30.72	5.12			25.60
		MegaBus	29.50			29.50	
		Balance c/d	84.78				
Total	175.00	Total	175.00	5.12	30.00	29.50	25.60

....

Task 11.7

(a)

Amount in petty cash box	£	91.70
Balance on petty cash control account	£	96.70
Difference	£	5.00

(b)

Petty cash reimbursement		
Date: 30.09.20XX		
Amount required to restore the cash in the petty cash box	£	240.24

....

Task 11.8

(a) – (b)

Petty cash book

Debit side		Credit side					
Details	Amount £	Details	Amount £	VAT £	Postage £	Travel £	Stationery £
Balance b/f	150.00	Tom's Taxi	18.00			18.00	
		Post Office	30.00		30.00		
		SMP Stationery	43.20	7.20			36.00
		Balance c/d	58.80				
Total	150.00	Total	150.00	7.20	30.00	18.00	36.00

Task 11.9

(a)

Amount in petty cash box	£	116.15
Balance on petty cash control account	£	120.00
Difference	£	3.85

(b)

Petty cash reimbursement		
Date: 31.07.20XX		
Amount required to restore the cash in the petty cash box	£	196.55

Task 11.10

(a) General ledger

Account name	Amount £	Debit ✓	Credit ✓
Petty cash	108.32		✓
VAT	15.52	✓	
Office expenses	15.20	✓	
Stationery	32.60	✓	
Maintenance	45.00	✓	

(b) The answer is: Petty cash

Tutorial note. The credit entry to petty cash would not be needed if the petty cash book was itself part of the general ledger double entry system.

Task 11.11

	✓
Imprest system	
Non-imprest system	✓

Task 11.12

(a) – (b)

Petty cash book

Debit side		Credit side					
Details	Amount £	Details	Amount £	VAT £	Postage £	Travel £	Stationery £
Balance b/f	75.23	Taxi	9.00			9.00	
Bank	60.00	Post Office	15.00		15.00		
		Suzie's Stationery	43.20	7.20			36.00
Balance b/d		Balance c/d	68.03				
Total	135.23	Total	135.23	7.20	15.00	9.00	36.00

(c) The correct answer is: £68.03

Tutorial note. The balance c/d on the petty cash book above is the amount of cash remaining in the petty cash tin on Friday. This is a **non-imprest** system of managing petty cash because Lucy tops up the balance by £60 each week independently of the petty cash expenditure.

Task 11.13

(a) – (b)

Petty cash-book

Details	Amount £	Details	Amount £	VAT £	Postage £	Stationery £
Balance b/f	175.00	Printer cartridges	17.40	2.90		14.50
		Stamps	12.60		12.60	
		Staplers	18.90	3.15		15.75
		Balance c/d	126.10			
Total	175.00	Totals	175.00	6.05	12.60	30.25

Working: £18.90 × 20/120 = £3.15 VAT

(c)

General ledger accounts	
Stamps	
Stationery	✓
Petty cash-book	
Petty cash control	
Postage	✓
Staplers	
VAT	✓

(d)

Remittance advice note	
Cheque requisition form	✓
Petty cash claim	
Customer statement	

(e) The correct answer is: £48.90 (£17.40 + £12.60 + £18.90)

(f) The correct answer is: No, there is not enough cash in the petty cash box

Chapter 12

Task 12.1

Ledger account	Balance	Debit ✓	Credit ✓
Sales	592,513		✓
Telephone	1,295	✓	
Sales ledger control	52,375	✓	
Wages	104,288	✓	
Purchases returns	8,229		✓
Bank overdraft	17,339		✓
Purchases	372,589	✓	
Drawings	71,604	✓	
Sales returns	32,800	✓	
Car	14,700	✓	
Purchases ledger control	31,570		✓

Task 12.2

	£	Debit £	Credit £
Office equipment		36,440	
Purchases		196,800	
Motor vehicles	76,800	76,800	
Sales	285,600		285,600
Bank (overdraft)	2,016		2,016
Petty cash	36	36	
Capital	90,000		90,000
Sales returns	5,640	5,640	
Purchases returns	4,320		4,320
Sales ledger control	42,960	42,960	
Purchases ledger control	36,120		36,120
VAT (owed to HMRC)	15,540		15,540
Drawings	12,040	12,040	
Telephone	1,920	1,920	
Electricity	3,360	3,360	
Wages	74,520	74,520	
Loan from bank	36,000		36,000
Discounts allowed	7,680	7,680	
Discounts received	4,680		4,680
Rent expense	16,080	16,080	
Totals		474,276	474,276

Task 12.3

Debit balances	Credit balances	✓
Assets and expenses	Liabilities, capital and income	✓

Task 12.4

The correct answer is: a liability or income

Task 12.5

The correct answer is: bank overdraft

Task 12.6

	£	Debit £	Credit £
Bank (overdraft)	4,838		4,838
Capital	216,000		216,000
Discounts allowed	18,432	18,432	
Discounts received	11,232		11,232
Drawings	28,896	28,896	
Electricity	8,064	8,064	
Loan from bank	86,400		86,400
Motor vehicles	184,320	184,320	
Office equipment	87,456	87,456	
Petty cash	100	100	
Purchases	472,320	472,320	
Purchases ledger control	86,688		86,688
Purchases returns	10,368		10,368
Rent expense	38,592	38,592	
Sales	685,440		685,440
Sales ledger control	103,104	103,104	
Sales returns	13,536	13,536	
Telephone	4,608	4,608	
VAT (owed to HMRC)	37,310		37,310
Wages	178,848	178,848	
Totals		1,138,276	1,138,276

AAT AQ2016 SAMPLE ASSESSMENT
Bookkeeping Transactions

Time allowed: 2 hours

Bookkeeping Transactions
AAT sample assessment

Introduction

The tasks in this assessment are set in different business situations where the following apply:

All businesses use a manual bookkeeping system.

Double entry takes place in the general ledger. Individual accounts of trade receivables and trade payables are kept in the sales and purchases ledgers as subsidiary accounts.

The cash book and petty cash book should be treated as part of the double entry system unless the task instructions state otherwise.

The VAT rate is 20%.

Task 1 (12 marks)

A sales invoice is being prepared for goods supplied, as shown in the customer order below.

Customer order

JABC Ltd
Order number 3971
Please supply: 12 March 20XX
120 units of product JBZ
@ £3.60 each less 7.5% trade discount.

(a) Calculate the amounts to be included in the invoice.

	£
Net amount before discount	
Net amount after discount	
VAT	
Total	

(b) **What will be the amounts entered in the sales daybook when the invoice in (a) has been prepared?**

Sales daybook

Date 20XX	Details	Invoice number	Total £	VAT £	Net £
12 Mar	JABC Ltd	1320			

A cheque for £1,567 has been received from JABC Ltd which they incorrectly state is in full settlement of the account at 28 February. The customer's account in the sales ledger is shown below.

JABC Ltd

Date 20XX	Details	Amount £	Date 20XX	Details	Amount £
1 Feb	Balance b/f	1,349	1 Feb	Credit note 88	480
8 Feb	Invoice 1223	270	4 Feb	Bank	869
17 Feb	Invoice 1250	1,208	13 Feb	Credit note 91	32
23 Feb	Invoice 1268	391	25 Feb	Credit note 96	110
28 Feb	Invoice 1281	3,420			

(c) **Show which THREE transactions are still outstanding by circling the relevant transactions below.**

Transactions

Balance b/f	Invoice 1223	Invoice 1250	Invoice 1268	Invoice 1281
	Credit note 88	Bank	Credit note 91	Credit note 96

A quotation to supply goods for £3,550.00 plus VAT has been sent to JABC Ltd offering a prompt payment discount of 2% for payment within 10 days.

(d) **What will be the amount JABC Ltd will pay if they purchase the goods and pay within 10 days?**

£ [ ]

Task 2 (9 marks)

The invoice and purchase order below relate to goods received from ABC Ltd.

Invoice

ABC Ltd	
VAT Registration number 369 4453 00	
Invoice No. 2178	
To: P Hill	15 April 20XX
	£
450 product code LL29 @ £1.20 each	540.00
VAT @ 20%	108.00
Total	648.00
Terms: Net monthly account	

Purchase order

P Hill
Order PO432

To: ABC Ltd   10 April 20XX

Please supply:

400 product code LL29 @ £1.20 each less 5% trade discount.

As agreed, terms of payment are 3% discount for payment by the end of the month.

(a) Identify any discrepancies on the invoice by drawing a line from each left hand box to the appropriate right hand box.

Terms of payment	Not shown on invoice
VAT rate	Incorrectly shown on invoice
Trade discount	Correctly shown on invoice
Quantity	

The invoice below has been received from Benton plc.

Invoice

Benton plc
VAT Registration number 436 4472 01

Invoice No. 13985

To: P Hill	15 April 20XX
	£
225 product code XX42 @	
£0.95 each	213.75
VAT @ 20%	42.75
Total	256.50

Terms: Net monthly account

(b) **Record the invoice in the appropriate daybook by:**

- **Selecting the correct daybook title and**
- **Making the necessary entries**.

Drop-down list:
Discounts allowed daybook
Discounts received daybook
Purchases daybook
Purchases returns daybook
Sales daybook
Sales returns daybook

Date 20XX	Details	Invoice number	Total £	VAT £	Net £
15 Apr	▼	13985			

Drop-down list:
Benton plc
P Hill

Task 3 (9 marks)

It is the policy of Cross plc to check statements of account when they are received and pay only those transactions that are included in the supplier's account in the purchases ledger. This is the account of DBL Ltd in the purchases ledger and the statement of account received from them.

(a) **Place a tick next to the three items in the statement of account that are not to be paid because they are missing from the supplier's account.**

DBL Ltd

Date 20XX	Details	Amount £	Date 20XX	Details	Amount £
1 Jun	Credit note C33	150	1 Jun	Balance b/f	12,946
4 Jun	Bank	12,946	10 Jun	Invoice 3921	462
			15 Jun	Invoice 4003	9,216
			21 Jun	Invoice 4079	1,543

Statement of account

DBL Ltd
149 Field Road, Darton, DF12 8GH

STATEMENT OF ACCOUNT

To: Cross plc   30 June 20XX

Date 20XX	Invoice/credit note number	Details	Amount £	Not to be paid ✓
1 Jun	C33	Goods returned	150	☐
10 Jun	3921	Goods	462	☐
15 Jun	4003	Goods	9,216	☐
16 Jun	C37	Goods returned	129	☐
17 Jun	4034	Goods	1,187	☐
21 Jun	4079	Goods	1,543	☐
29 Jun	4170	Goods	3,926	☐

(b) **What will be the amount paid?**

£ _____

This is the account of Stone plc in the purchases ledger and a credit note that has been received from the supplier but not yet entered into their account.

Stone plc

Date 20XX	Details	Amount £	Date 20XX	Details	Amount £
1 Jul	Bank	3,684	1 Jul	Balance b/f	3,882
1 Jul	Credit note S74	482	3 Jul	Invoice S2227	917
			4 Jul	Invoice S2243	1,446
			4 Jul	Invoice S2260	352

Credit note

```
              Stone plc
VAT Registration number 412 3297 00

         Credit note No. S81

To: Cross plc              5 July 20XX

                              £

To correct overcharge on Invoice
   S2156                    165.00
VAT @ 20%                    33.00
Total                       198.00

     Terms: Net monthly account
```

(c) **What will be the amount to be paid to Stone plc once the credit note has been entered into their account?**

£ _____

The two invoices below were received on 6 July from credit suppliers who offer a prompt payment discount.

Invoice

```
              Baker plc
VAT Registration number 569 4453 01

        Invoice No. 2199

To: Cross plc              5 July 20XX

                              £
45 product code XX29 @
     £25.00 each          1,125.00
VAT @ 20%                   225.00
Total                     1,350.00

Terms: 2% discount if payment received
   within 10 days of date of invoice.
```

Invoice

```
             Goodwin Ltd
VAT Registration number 442 6753 00

        Invoice No. G289

To: Cross plc              5 July 20XX

                              £
200 product code Z4G @
     £13.25 each          2,650.00
VAT @ 20%                   530.00
Total                     3,180.00

Terms: 2.5% discount if payment received
   within 14 days of date of invoice.
```

(d) Calculate the amount to be paid to each supplier if the discount is taken and show the date by which the supplier should receive the payment.

Supplier	£	Date by which payment should be received by supplier
Baker plc		▼
Goodwin Ltd		▼

Drop-down list:

5 July 20XX
6 July 20XX
15 July 20XX
16 July 20XX
19 July 20XX
20 July 20XX

Task 4 (15 marks)

The two amounts shown below have been received from customers and are ready to be entered in the cash book.

Burgess Retail Remittance advice
1 August 20XX
An amount of £474 will be transferred to your bank account today by BACS, in full settlement of our June account.

Receipt 108
1 August 20XX
Cheque for £1,000 and cash £326 received from Alba plc for goods supplied today – £1,326 including VAT.

(a) Make the necessary entries in the cash book and total each column.

Cash book – debit side

Details	Cash £	Bank £	VAT £	Trade receivables £	Cash sales £
Balance b/f	183	3,220			
▼					
▼					
Totals					

Drop-down list:

Alba plc
Bank
Burgess Retail
Cash
Trade receivables
VAT

The credit side of the cash book shows total cash payments during the week were £342.

(b) Using your answer to (a), calculate the cash balance.

£ [   ]

The credit side of the cash book shows total bank payments during the week were £1,743.

(c) Using your answer to (a), calculate the bank balance. Use a minus sign if your calculations indicate an overdrawn bank balance, eg –123.

£ [   ]

Task 5 (15 marks)

The two petty cash vouchers below are ready to be entered into the partially completed petty cash book.

Petty cash voucher 136	
	31 August 20XX
	£
Postage stamps	32.29
VAT is not applicable.	

Petty cash voucher 137	
	31 August 20XX
	£
Motor repairs	25.50
VAT @ 20%	5.10
Total	30.60

(a) Complete the petty cash book by:

- **Entering both transactions into the petty cash book below.**

- **Totalling the petty cash book and inserting the balance carried down at 31 August.**

Petty cash book

Date 20XX	Details	Amount £	Date 20XX	Details	Amount £	VAT £	Motor expenses £	Office expenses £
24 Aug	Balance b/f	37.60	27 Aug	Stationery	23.46	3.91		19.55
24 Aug	Cash from bank	87.40	31 Aug	▼				
			31 Aug	▼				
			31 Aug	▼				
	Total			**Totals**				

Drop-down list:

Balance b/f
Balance c/d
Motor expenses
Motor repairs
Office expenses
Postage stamps
VAT

(b) **What will be the amount of cash withdrawn from the bank to restore the imprest level of £125.00?**

£ [   ]

Task 6 (12 marks)

These are the totals of the discounts allowed daybook at the end of the month.

Discounts allowed daybook

Details	Total £	VAT £	Net £
Totals	510	85	425

(a) **What will be the entries in the general ledger?**

Account name		Amount £	Debit ✓	Credit ✓
	▼			
	▼			
	▼			

Drop-down list:

Discounts allowed
Discounts received
Purchases
Purchases ledger control
Purchases returns
Sales
Sales ledger control
Sales returns
VAT

One of the entries in the discounts allowed daybook is for a credit note sent to Jackson Jones for £70 plus VAT.

(b)   What will be the entry in the sales ledger?

Account name		Amount £	Debit ✓	Credit ✓
	▼			

Drop-down list:

Discounts allowed
Discounts received
Jackson Jones
Purchases
Purchases ledger control
Purchases returns
Sales
Sales ledger control
Sales returns
VAT

Task 7 (12 marks)

These are totals of the cash book at the end of the month.

Cash book

Cash £	Bank £	VAT £	Trade receivables £	Cash sales £	Cash £	Bank £	VAT £	Trade payables £	Cash purchases £
854	16,370	------	16,370	------	854	16,370	59	9,942	295

What will be the entries in the general ledger?

Account name		Amount £	Debit ✓	Credit ✓
	▼			
	▼			
	▼			
	▼			

Drop-down list:

Bank
Cash
Cash purchases
Cash sales
Purchases ledger control
Sales ledger control
VAT

....

Task 8 (12 marks)

The following two accounts are in the general ledger at close of day on 31 October.

Loan from bank

Date 20XX	Details	Amount £	Date 20XX	Details	Amount £
15 Oct	Bank	1,270	1 Oct	Balance b/f	26,725
			31 Oct	Bank	10,000

Office equipment

Date 20XX	Details	Amount £	Date 20XX	Details	Amount £
1 Oct	Balance b/f	13,924	30 Oct	Journal	200
8 Oct	Bank	865			

(a) What will be the balance brought down at 1 November on each account?

Account	Balance b/d at 1 November	Debit ✓	Credit ✓
Loan from bank			
Office equipment			

The following account is in the sales ledger at the close of day on 31 October.

(b) Complete the account below by:

- Inserting the balance carried down together with date and details.
- Inserting the totals.
- Inserting the balance brought down together with date and details.

Zahra Zee

Date 20XX	Details	Amount £	Date 20XX	Details	Amount £
1 Oct	Balance b/f	14,264	22 Oct	Bank	1,525
11 Oct	Invoice 3225	977	29 Oct	Credit Note C112	3,714
▼	▼		▼	▼	
	Total			Total	
▼	▼		▼	▼	

Drop-down list:

1 Nov
31 Oct
Balance b/d
Balance c/d
Zahra Zee

Task 9 (12 marks)

Below are two general ledger accounts and a partially completed trial balance.

Complete the trial balance by:

- Transferring the balances of the two general ledger accounts to the debit or credit column of the trial balance.
- Entering the amounts shown against each of the other account names into the debit or credit column of the trial balance.
- Totalling both columns of the trial balance

Do not enter figures with decimal places in this task and do not enter a zero in unused column cells.

Sales

Date 20XX	Details	Amount £	Date 20XX	Details	Amount £
30 Nov	Journal	625	1 Nov	Balance b/f	60,886
30 Nov	Balance c/d	80,700	30 Nov	Sales ledger control	20,439
		81,325			81,325

Purchases

Date 20XX	Details	Amount £	Date 20XX	Details	Amount £
1 Nov	Balance b/f	29,475	30 Nov	Balance c/d	40,872
30 Nov	Purchases ledger control	11,397			
		40,872			40,872

Trial balance as at 30 November

Account name	Amount £	Debit £	Credit £
Sales			
Purchases			
Administration expenses	5,791		
Bank (overdraft)	5,000		
Motor vehicle	32,734		
Motor expenses	1,392		
Sales ledger control	19,433		
Purchase ledger control	10,480		
Rent and rates	2,250		
Capital	6,292		
Totals			

Task 10 (12 marks)

A new business has allocated a customer account code to each customer in the sales ledger, as shown below. The code is made up of the first four letters of the customer's name, followed by the number of the ledger page allocated to each customer in that alphabetical group.

Customer name	Customer account code
Aspen Ltd	ASPE01
Attwood Ltd	ATTW02
Dunston Designs	DUNS01
Genie Products	GENI01

Customer name	Customer account code
Latham Ltd	LATH01
Pemberton Ltd	PEMB01
Penn Ltd	PENN02

The two new customer accounts shown below have been added to the sales ledger and need to be allocated a customer account code.

(a) Insert the relevant account codes for each customer.

Hartstone plc   Account code: [   ]   Parker Printing   Account code: [   ]

Date 20XX	Details	Amount £	Date 20XX	Details	Amount £	Date 20XX	Details	Amount £	Date 20XX	Details	Amount £
3 Dec	Invoice 115	628				3 Dec	Invoice 116	943			

One customer has been offered a prompt payment discount for payment within 10 days.

(b) Show what TWO actions should be taken if the customer takes the discount and pays within 10 days.

Action	✓
Record the amount received in the cash book and ledgers.	
Change the amounts of the original invoice.	
Issue a new invoice for the amount paid.	
Issue a credit note for the discount taken plus VAT.	

The business has the following assets and liabilities.

Assets and liabilities	£
Premises	115,000
Loan from bank	45,000
Cash at bank	11,433
Furniture and fittings	12,392
Amounts owing to credit suppliers	22,396
Amounts owing from credit customers	14,224

(c) **Show the accounting equation by inserting the appropriate figures.**

Assets £	Liabilities £	Capital £

The transactions below have taken place.

(d) **Show whether each transaction will be classified as capital expenditure, capital income, revenue expenditure or revenue income by placing the appropriate classification against each transaction in the table below. You can use each classification more than once.**

Transaction	Classification
Purchased motor van for delivery of goods.	
Purchased stationery for use in the office.	
Purchased train tickets for business travel.	
Received cash for the sale of goods.	
Received a cheque from the owner.	

Classification:

Capital expenditure

Capital income

Revenue expenditure

Revenue income

AAT AQ2016 SAMPLE ASSESSMENT
Bookkeeping Transactions

ANSWERS

Bookkeeping Transactions
AAT sample assessment

Task 1 (12 marks)

(a) Calculate the amounts to be included in the invoice.

	£
Net amount before discount	432.00
Net amount after discount	399.60
VAT	79.92
Total	479.52

(b) What will be the amounts entered in the sales daybook when the invoice in (a) has been prepared?

Sales daybook

Date 20XX	Details	Invoice number	Total £	VAT £	Net £
12 Mar	JABC Ltd	1320	479.52	79.92	399.60

(c) Show which THREE transactions are still outstanding by circling the relevant transactions below.

Transactions
Balance b/f   (Invoice 1223)   Invoice 1250   Invoice 1268   (Invoice 1281)
Credit note 88   Bank   Credit note 91   (Credit note 96)

A quotation to supply goods for £3,550.00 plus VAT has been sent to JABC Ltd offering a prompt payment discount of 2% for payment within 10 days.

(d) What will be the amount JABC Ltd will pay if they purchase the goods and pay within 10 days?

£ | 4,174.80 |

· ·

Task 2 (9 marks)

(a) Identify any discrepancies on the invoice by drawing a line from each left hand box to the appropriate right hand box.

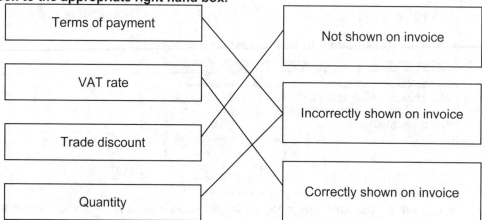

(b) Record the invoice in the appropriate daybook by:

- Selecting the correct daybook title and
- Making the necessary entries.

Purchases daybook ▼

Date 20XX	Details	Invoice number	Total £	VAT £	Net £
15 Apr	Benton plc ▼	13985	256.50	42.75	213.75

Task 3 (9 marks)

(a) **Statement of account**

	DBL Ltd			
	149 Field Road, Darton, DF12 8GH			
	STATEMENT OF ACCOUNT			

To: Cross plc   30 June 20XX

Date 20XX	Invoice/credit note number	Details	Amount £	Not to be paid ✓
1 Jun	C33	Goods returned	150	☐
10 Jun	3921	Goods	462	☐
15 Jun	4003	Goods	9,216	☐
16 Jun	C37	Goods returned	129	☑
17 Jun	4034	Goods	1,187	☑
21 Jun	4079	Goods	1,543	☐
29 Jun	4170	Goods	3,926	☑

(b) **What will be the amount paid?**

£ 11,071

(c) **What will be the amount to be paid to Stone plc once the credit note has been entered into their account?**

£ 2,233

(d) **Calculate the amount to be paid to each supplier if the discount is taken and show the date by which the supplier should receive the payment.**

Supplier	£	Date by which payment should be received by supplier	
Baker plc	1,323.00	15 July 20XX	▼
Goodwin Ltd	3,100.50	19 July 20XX	▼

Task 4 (15 marks)

(a) Make the necessary entries in the cash book and total each column.

Cash book – debit side

Details	Cash £	Bank £	VAT £	Trade receivables £	Cash sales £
Balance b/f	183	3,220			
Burgess Retail ▼		474		474	
Alba plc ▼	326	1,000	221		1,105
Totals	509	4,694	221	474	1,105

The credit side of the cash book shows total cash payments during the week were £342.

(b) Using your answer to (a), calculate the cash balance.

£ 167

The credit side of the cash book shows total bank payments during the week were £1,743.

(c) Using your answer to (a), calculate the bank balance. Use a minus sign if your calculations indicate an overdrawn bank balance, eg –123.

£ 2,951

Task 5 (15 marks)

(a) Complete the petty cash book by:

• Entering both transactions into the petty cash book below.

• Totalling the petty cash book and inserting the balance carried down at 31 August.

Petty cash book

Date 20XX	Details	Amount £	Date 20XX	Details	Amount £	VAT £	Motor expenses £	Office expenses £
24 Aug	Balance b/f	37.60	27 Aug	Stationery	23.46	3.91		19.55
24 Aug	Cash from bank	87.40	31 Aug	Postage stamps ▼	32.29			32.29
			31 Aug	Motor repairs ▼	30.60	5.10	25.50	
			31 Aug	Balance c/d ▼	38.65			
	Total	125.00		Totals	125.00	9.01	25.50	51.84

(b) **What will be the amount of cash withdrawn from the bank to restore the imprest level of £125.00?**

£ | 86.35 |

Task 6 (12 marks)

(a) **What will be the entries in the general ledger?**

Account name		Amount £	Debit ✓	Credit ✓
Discounts allowed	▼	425	✓	
VAT	▼	85	✓	
Sales ledger control	▼	510		✓

One of the entries in the discounts allowed daybook is for a credit note sent to Jackson Jones for £70 plus VAT.

(b) **What will be the entry in the sales ledger?**

Account name		Amount £	Debit ✓	Credit ✓
Jackson Jones	▼	84		✓

Task 7 (12 marks)

What will be the entries in the general ledger?

Account name		Amount £	Debit ✓	Credit ✓
VAT	▼	59	✓	
Purchases ledger control	▼	9,942	✓	
Cash purchases	▼	295	✓	
Sales ledger control	▼	16,370		✓

Task 8 (12 marks)

(a) What will be the balance brought down at 1 November on each amount?

Account	Balance b/d at 1 November	Debit	Credit
Loan from bank	35,455		✓
Office equipment	14,589	✓	

The following account is in the sales ledger at the close of day on 31 October.

(b) Complete the account below by:

- Inserting the balance carried down together with date and details.
- Inserting the totals.
- Inserting the balance brought down together with date and details.

Zahra Zee

Date 20XX	Details	Amount £	Date 20XX	Details	Amount £
1 Oct	Balance b/f	14,264	22 Oct	Bank	1,525
11 Oct	Invoice 3225	977	29 Oct	Credit Note C112	3,714
	▾		31 Oct	Balance c/d ▾	10,002
	Total	15,241		Total	15,241
1 Nov	Balance b/d ▾	10,002		▾	

Task 9 (12 marks)

Trial balance as at 30 November

Account name	Amount £	Debit £	Credit £
Sales			80,700
Purchases		40,872	
Administration expenses	5,791	5,791	
Bank (overdraft)	5,000		5,000
Motor vehicle	32,734	32,734	
Motor expenses	1,392	1,392	
Sales ledger control	19,433	19,433	
Purchase ledger control	10,480		10,480
Rent and rates	2,250	2,250	
Capital	6,292		6,292
Totals		102,472	102,472

Task 10 (12 marks)

(a) Insert the relevant account codes for each customer.

Hartstone plc   Account code: | HART01 | Parker Printing   Account code: | PARK03 |

Date 20XX	Details	Amount £	Date 20XX	Details	Amount £	Date 20XX	Details	Amount £	Date 20XX	Details	Amount £
3 Dec	Invoice 115	628				3 Dec	Invoice 116	943			

One customer has been offered a prompt payment discount for payment within 10 days.

(b) Show what TWO actions should be taken if the customer takes the discount and pays within 10 days.

Action	✓
Record the amount received in the cash book and ledgers.	✓
Change the amounts of the original invoice.	
Issue a new invoice for the amount paid.	
Issue a credit note for the discount taken plus VAT.	✓

(c) **Show the accounting equation by inserting the appropriate figures.**

Assets £	Liabilities £	Capital £
153,049	67,396	85,653

The transaction below has taken place.

(d) **Show whether each transaction will be classified as capital expenditure, capital income, revenue expenditure or revenue income by placing the appropriate classification against each transaction in the table below. You can use each classification more than once.**

Transaction	Classification
Purchased motor van for delivery of goods.	Capital expenditure
Purchased stationery for use in the office.	Revenue expenditure
Purchased train tickets for business travel.	Revenue expenditure
Received cash for the sale of goods.	Revenue income
Received a cheque from the owner.	Capital income

Classification:

Classification:
Capital expenditure
Capital income
Revenue expenditure
Revenue income

BPP PRACTICE ASSESSMENT 1
Bookkeeping Transactions

Time allowed: 2 hours

Bookkeeping Transactions
BPP practice assessment 1

Introduction

The tasks in this assessment are set in different business situations where the following apply:

All businesses use a manual bookkeeping system.

Double entry takes place in the general ledger. Individual accounts of trade receivables and trade payables are kept in the sales and purchases ledgers as subsidiary accounts.

The cash book and petty cash book should be treated as part of the double entry system unless the task instructions state otherwise.

The VAT rate is 20%.

Task 1

A sales invoice is being prepared for goods supplied, as shown in the customer order below.

Customer order

Jules Ltd
Order number 1739
Please supply: 18 April 20XX
55 units of product C54
@ £13 each less 10% trade discount.

(a)   Calculate the amounts to be included in the invoice.

	£
Net amount before discount	
Net amount after discount	
VAT	
Total	

(b)   What will be the amounts entered in the sales daybook when the invoice in (a) has been prepared?

Sales daybook

Date 20XX	Details	Invoice number	Total £	VAT £	Net £
18 Apr	Jules Ltd	621			

A cheque for £1,287 has been received from Jules Ltd which they incorrectly state is in full settlement of the account at 31 May. The customer's account in the sales ledger is shown below.

Jules Ltd

Date 20XX	Details	Amount £	Date 20XX	Details	Amount £
1 May	Balance b/f	652	1 May	Credit note 7	120
8 May	Invoice 52	301	4 May	Bank	532
17 May	Invoice 63	1,001	13 May	Credit note 11	15
23 May	Invoice 65	251	25 May	Credit note 13	99
28 May	Invoice 66	2,639			

(c) **Show which THREE transactions are still outstanding by circling the relevant transactions below.**

Transactions

Balance b/f   Invoice 52   Invoice 63   Invoice 65   Invoice 66

Credit note 7   Bank   Credit note 11   Credit note 13

A quotation to supply goods for £11,390.00 plus VAT has been sent to Jules Ltd offering a prompt payment discount of 3% for payment within 14 days.

(d) **What will be the amount Jules Ltd will pay if they purchase the goods and pay within 14 days?**

£ [   ]

Task 2

The invoice and purchase order below relate to goods received from XYZ Ltd.

Invoice

XYZ Ltd
VAT Registration number 963 5353 01

Invoice No. 8753

To: B Smith	19 May 20XX

	£
50 product code 5357 @ £5 each	250.00
Trade discount @10%	25.00
Total	225.00

Terms: 3% discount for payment within 10 days

Purchase order

B Smith
Order PO432

To: XYZ Ltd	13 May 20XX

Please supply:

100 product code 5357 @ £5 each less 10% trade discount.

As agreed, terms of payment are 3% discount for payment within 10 days

(a) Identify any discrepancies on the invoice by drawing a line from each left hand box to the appropriate right hand box.

Terms of payment

VAT rate

Trade discount

Quantity

Not shown on invoice

Incorrectly shown on invoice

Correctly shown on invoice

The invoice below has been received from Clinton plc.

Invoice

Clinton plc
VAT Registration number 896 5421 01
Invoice No. 6532

To: B Smith   19 May 20XX

	£
5 product code 952 @	
£15.35 each	76.75
VAT @ 20%	15.35
Total	92.10

Terms: 4% discount for payment in
10 days

(b) **Record the invoice in the appropriate daybook by:**

- **selecting the correct daybook title and**
- **making the necessary entries**.

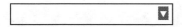

Picklist:
Discounts allowed daybook
Discounts received daybook
Purchases daybook
Purchases returns daybook
Sales daybook
Sales returns daybook

Date 20XX	Details	Invoice number	Total £	VAT £	Net £
19 May	▼	6532			

Picklist:
B Smith
Clinton plc

Task 3

It is the policy of Rigley plc to check statements of account when they are received and pay only those transactions that are included in the supplier's account in the purchases ledger. This is the account of Rowley Ltd in the purchases ledger and the statement of account received from them.

(a) Place a tick next to the three items in the statement of account that are not to be paid because they are missing from the supplier's account.

Rowley Ltd

Date 20XX	Details	Amount £	Date 20XX	Details	Amount £
1 Sept	Credit note C25	75	1 Sept	Balance b/f	15,895
4 Sept	Bank	15,895	10 Sept	Invoice 321	501
			15 Sept	Invoice 333	1,365
			29 Sept	Invoice 378	2,300

Statement of account

Rowley Ltd
34 Allridge Way, Rigby DF12 8GH

STATEMENT OF ACCOUNT

To: Rigley plc   30 Sept 20XX

Date 20XX	Invoice/credit note number	Details	Amount £	Not to be paid ✓
1 Sept	C25	Goods returned	75	☐
10 Sept	321	Goods	501	☐
15 Sept	333	Goods	1,365	☐
16 Sept	C26	Goods returned	55	☐
17 Sept	334	Goods	894	☐
21 Sept	371	Goods	1,654	☐
29 Sept	378	Goods	2,300	☐

(b) What will be the amount paid?

£ [   ]

This is the account of Pebble plc in the purchases ledger and a credit note that has been received from the supplier but not yet entered into their account.

Pebble plc

Date 20XX	Details	Amount £	Date 20XX	Details	Amount £
1 Oct	Bank	1,532	1 Oct	Balance b/f	4,527
1 Oct	Credit note C53	653	3 Oct	Invoice I592	891
			4 Oct	Invoice I699	998
			4 Oct	Invoice I703	1,452

Credit note

```
                    Pebble plc
        VAT Registration number 412 3297 00

            Credit note No. C65

To: Rigley plc                    5 Oct 20XX

                                      £
To correct overcharge on Invoice
    I589                           89.00
VAT @ 20%                          17.80
Total                             106.80

        Terms: Net monthly account
```

(c) **What will be the amount to be paid to Pebble plc once the credit note has been entered into their account?**

£ _____

The two invoices below were received on 6 October from credit suppliers who offer a prompt payment discount.

Invoice

Babby plc	
VAT Registration number 569 4453 01	
Invoice No. 9932	
To: Rigley plc	5 Oct 20XX
	£
4 product code XX29 @ £250.00 each	1,000.00
VAT @ 20%	200.00
Total	1,200.00

Terms: 3% discount if payment received within 14 days of date of invoice.

Invoice

Hague Ltd	
VAT Registration number 442 6753 00	
Invoice No. H321	
To: Rigley plc	5 Oct 20XX
	£
2000 product code Z4G @ £1.25 each	2,500.00
VAT @ 20%	500.00
Total	3,000.00

Terms: 3.5% discount if payment received within 10 days of date of invoice.

(d) Calculate the amount to be paid to each supplier if the discount is taken and show the date by which the supplier should receive the payment.

Supplier	£	Date by which payment should be received by supplier
Babby plc		▼
Hague Ltd		▼

Picklist:

5 October 20XX
6 October 20XX
15 October 20XX
16 October 20XX
19 October 20XX
20 October 20XX

Task 4

The two amounts shown below have been received from customers and are ready to be entered in the cash book.

<table>
<tr><td>

Receipt 56

1 November 20XX

Cheque for £500 and cash £124 received from Beta plc for goods supplied today – £624 including VAT.

</td><td>

Bally Designs
Remittance advice

1 November 20XX

An amount of £535 will be transferred to your bank account today by BACS, in full settlement of our September account.

</td></tr>
</table>

(a) **Make the necessary entries in the cash book and total each column.**

Cash book – debit side

Details	Cash £	Bank £	VAT £	Trade receivables £	Cash sales £
Balance b/f	183	3,220			
▼					
▼					
Totals					

Picklist:

Bally Designs
Bank
Beta plc
Cash
Trade receivables
VAT

The credit side of the cash book shows total cash payments during the week were £256.

(b) **Using your answer to (a), calculate the cash balance.**

£ [   ]

The credit side of the cash book shows total bank payments during the week were £1,743.

(c) **Using your answer to (a), calculate the bank balance. Use a minus sign if your calculations indicate an overdrawn bank balance, eg –123.**

£ [   ]

Task 5

The two petty cash vouchers below are ready to be entered into the partially completed petty cash book.

Petty cash voucher 255	
	31 October 20XX
	£
Motor repairs	42.50
VAT is not applicable.	

Petty cash voucher 256	
	31 October 20XX
	£
Printer paper	15.50
VAT @ 20%	3.10
Total	18.60

(a) **Complete the petty cash book by:**

- **Entering both transactions into the petty cash book below.**

- **Totalling the petty cash book and inserting the balance carried down at 31 October.**

Petty cash book

Date 20XX	Details	Amount £	Date 20XX	Details	Amount £	VAT £	Motor expenses £	Office expenses £
24 Oct	Balance b/f	37.60	27 Oct	Postage stamps	5.45			5.45
24 Oct	Cash from bank	72.40	31 Oct	▼				
			31 Oct	▼				
			31 Oct	▼				
	Total			**Totals**				

Picklist:

Balance b/f
Balance c/d
Motor expenses
Motor repairs
Office expenses
Stationery
VAT

(b) **What will be the amount of cash withdrawn from the bank to restore the imprest level of £110.00?**

£ [ ]

Task 6

These are the totals of the discounts allowed daybook at the end of the month.

Discounts allowed daybook

Details	Total £	VAT £	Net £
Totals	378	63	315

(a) **What will be the entries in the general ledger?**

Account name	Amount £	Debit ✓	Credit ✓
▼			
▼			
▼			

Picklist:

Discounts allowed
Discounts received
Purchases
Purchases ledger control
Purchases returns
Sales
Sales ledger control
Sales returns
VAT

One of the entries in the discounts allowed daybook is for a credit note sent to Samuel Smith for £112 plus VAT.

(b) **What will be the entry in the sales ledger?**

Account name	Amount £	Debit ✓	Credit ✓
▼			

Picklist:

Discounts allowed
Discounts received
Purchases
Purchases ledger control
Purchases returns
Sales
Sales ledger control
Sales returns
Samuel Smith
VAT

Task 7

These are totals of the cash book at the end of the month.

Cash book

Cash £	Bank £	VAT £	Trade receivables £	Cash sales £	Cash £	Bank £	VAT £	Trade payables £	Cash purchases £
657	8,255	------	8,255	--------	657	8,255	63	5,450	295

What will be the entries in the general ledger?

Account name		Amount £	Debit ✓	Credit ✓
	▼			
	▼			
	▼			
	▼			

Picklist:

Bank
Cash
Cash purchases
Cash sales
Purchases ledger control
Sales ledger control
VAT

....

Task 8

The following two accounts are in the general ledger at close of day on 31 January.

Loan from bank

Date 20XX	Details	Amount £	Date 20XX	Details	Amount £
15 Jan	Bank	3,050	1 Jan	Balance b/f	36,525
			31 Jan	Bank	20,000

Motor Vehicles

Date 20XX	Details	Amount £	Date 20XX	Details	Amount £
1 Jan	Balance b/f	32,900	30 Jan	Journal	500
8 Jan	Bank	2,500			

(a) **What will be the balance brought down at 1 February on each account?**

Account	Balance b/d at 1 February	Debit ✓	Credit ✓
Loan from bank			
Motor Vehicles			

The following account is in the sales ledger at the close of day on 31 January.

(b) **Complete the account below by:**

- **Inserting the balance carried down together with date and details.**
- **Inserting the totals.**
- **Inserting the balance brought down together with date and details.**

Trevor Tate

Date 20XX	Details	Amount £	Date 20XX	Details	Amount £
1 Jan	Balance b/f	9,899	22 Jan	Bank	5,780
11 Jan	Invoice 155	1,001	29 Jan	Credit Note C15	3,714
▼		▼	▼		▼
	Total			Total	
▼		▼	▼		▼

Picklist:

1 Feb
31 Jan
Balance b/d
Balance c/d
Trevor Tate

Task 9

Below are two general ledger accounts and a partially completed trial balance.

Complete the trial balance by:

- **Transferring the balances of the two general ledger accounts to the debit or credit column of the trial balance.**
- **Entering the amounts shown against each of the other account names into the debit or credit column of the trial balance.**
- **Totalling both columns of the train balance**

Do not enter figures with decimal places in this task and do not enter a zero in unused column cells.

BPP
LEARNING MEDIA

Sales

Date 20XX	Details	Amount £	Date 20XX	Details	Amount £
31 Mar	Journal	350	1 Mar	Balance b/f	73,481
31 Mar	Balance c/d	91,500	31 Mar	Sales ledger control	18,369
		91,850			91,850

Purchases

Date 20XX	Details	Amount £	Date 20XX	Details	Amount £
1 Mar	Balance b/f	25,300	31 Mar	Balance c/d	34,156
31 Mar	Purchases ledger control	8,856			
		34,156			34,156

Trial balance as at 31 March

Account name	Amount £	Debit £	Credit £
Sales			
Purchases			
Administration expenses	8,965		
Bank (overdraft)	3,000		
Motor vehicle	35,505		
Motor expenses	1,392		
Sales ledger control	21,456		
Purchase ledger control	8,423		
Rent and rates	3,250		
Capital	1,801		
Totals			

Task 10

A new business has allocated a customer account code to each customer in the sales ledger, as shown below. The code is made up of the first four letters of the customer's name, followed by the number of the ledger page allocated to each customer in that alphabetical group.

Customer name	Customer account code
Aspen Ltd	ASPE01
Attwood Ltd	ATTW02
Dunston Designs	DUNS01
Genie Products	GENI01
Latham Ltd	LATH01
Pemberton Ltd	PEMB01
Penn Ltd	PENN02

The two new customer accounts shown below have been added to the sales ledger and need to be allocated a customer account code.

(a) Insert the relevant account codes for each customer.

General plc   Account code: [   ]   Mulitpack Ltd   Account code: [   ]

Date 20XX	Details	Amount £	Date 20XX	Details	Amount £	Date 20XX	Details	Amount £	Date 20XX	Details	Amount £
3 Dec	Invoice 115	628				3 Dec	Invoice 116	943			

A supplier has offered the company a prompt payment discount for payment within 14 days.

(b) Show what TWO events or actions would happen if the company chooses to take the discount and pays within 14 days.

Action	✓
Record the amount paid in the cash book and ledgers.	
Change the amounts of the original invoice in the purchases ledger.	
Receive a credit note for the discount taken plus VAT.	
Request a new invoice for the amount actually paid.	

The business has the following assets and liabilities.

Assets and liabilities	£
Premises	111,000
Loan from bank	5,000
Cash at bank	11,433
Motor Vehicles	15,390
Amounts owing to credit suppliers	22,446
Amounts owing from credit customers	11,233

(c) **Show the accounting equation by inserting the appropriate figures.**

Assets £	Liabilities £	Capital £

The transactions below have taken place.

(d) **Show whether each transaction will be classified as capital expenditure, capital income, revenue expenditure or revenue income by placing the appropriate classification against each transaction in the table below. You can use each classification more than once.**

Transaction	Classification
Purchased computers for use in the office.	
Purchased stationery for use in the office.	
Purchased a car for the sales person to use for business trips.	
Received cheque for the sale of goods.	
Sold a van the company owned.	

Classification:

Capital expenditure

Capital income

Revenue expenditure

Revenue income

BPP PRACTICE ASSESSMENT 1
Bookkeeping Transactions

ANSWERS

Bookkeeping Transactions
BPP practice assessment 1

Task 1

(a)

	£
Net amount before discount	715.00
Net amount after discount	643.50
VAT	128.70
Total	772.20

Tutorial note. Workings: Net before discount: 55 × £13 = £715, net after discount: £715 × 90% = £643.50, VAT: £643.50 × 20% = £128.7

(b) **Sales daybook**

Date 20XX	Details	Invoice number	Total £	VAT £	Net £
18 Apr	Jules Ltd	621	772.20	128.70	643.50

(c)

Transactions
Balance b/f   Invoice 52   Invoice 63   (Invoice 65)   (Invoice 66)
Credit note 7   Bank   Credit note 11   (Credit note 13)

Tutorial note. Working: £652 – £120 – £532 = 0; £301 + £1,001– £15 = £1,287

(d)   £ | 13,257.96 |

Tutorial note.
Working:

Gross: £11,390 + (£11,390 × 20%) = £13,668

Amount paid: £13,668 × 97% = £13,257.96

Task 2

(a)

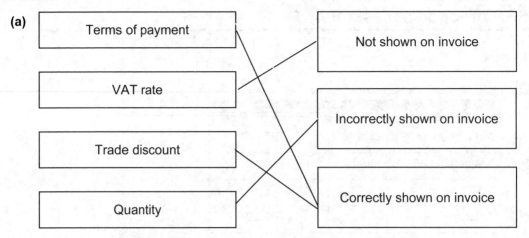

(b) Purchases daybook ▼

Date 20XX	Details	Invoice number	Total £	VAT £	Net £
19 May	Clinton plc ▼	6532	92.10	15.35	76.75

Task 3

Statement of account

(a)

Rowley Ltd
34 Allridge Way, Rigby DF12 8GH
STATEMENT OF ACCOUNT

To: Rigley plc   30 Sept 20XX

Date 20XX	Invoice/credit note number	Details	Amount £	Not to be paid ✓
1 Sept	C25	Goods returned	75	☐
10 Sept	321	Goods	501	☐
15 Sept	333	Goods	1,365	☐
16 Sept	C26	Goods returned	55	✓
17 Sept	334	Goods	894	✓
21 Sept	371	Goods	1,654	✓
29 Sept	378	Goods	2,300	☐

(b) £ 4,091

Tutorial note.

Working: £501 + £1,365 + £2,300 − £75 = £4,091

(c) £ 5,576.20

Tutorial note.

Working: £4,527 + £891 + £998 + £1,452 − £1,532 − £653 − £106.80 = £5,576.20

(d)

Supplier	£	Date by which payment should be received by supplier
Babby plc	1,164	19 October 20XX ▼
Hague Ltd	2,895	15 October 20XX ▼

Tutorial note.

Babby plc £1,200 × 97% = £1,164
Hague Ltd £3,000 × 96.5% = £2,895

Task 4

(a) Cash book – debit side

Details	Cash £	Bank £	VAT £	Trade receivables £	Cash sales £
Balance b/f	183	3,220			
Bally Designs		535		535	
Beta plc	124	500	104		520
Totals	307	4,255	104	535	520

(b) £ 51

Tutorial note.
Working: £307 – £256 = £51

(c) £ 2,512

Tutorial note.

Working: £4,255 – £1,743 = £2,512

Task 5

(a) Petty cash book

Date 20XX	Details	Amount £	Date 20XX	Details	Amount £	VAT £	Motor expenses £	Office expenses £
24 Oct	Balance b/f	37.60	27 Oct	Postage stamps	5.45			5.45
24 Oct	Cash from bank	72.40	31 Oct	Motor repairs ▼	42.50		42.50	
			31 Oct	Stationery ▼	18.60	3.10		15.50
			31 Oct	Balance c/d ▼	43.45			
	Total	110.00		Totals	110.00	3.10	42.50	20.95

(b) £ 66.55

Tutorial note.

Working: £5.45 + £42.50 + £18.60 = £66.55

Task 6

(a)

Account name	Amount £	Debit ✓	Credit ✓
Discounts allowed ▼	315	✓	
VAT ▼	63	✓	
Sales ledger control ▼	378		✓

(b) **What will be the entry in the sales ledger?**

Account name	Amount £	Debit ✓	Credit ✓
Samuel Smith ▼	134.4		✓

Tutorial note.

Working: £112 + (£112 × 20%) = £134.4

Task 7

Account name	Amount £	Debit ✓	Credit ✓
VAT ▼	63	✓	
Purchases ledger control ▼	5,450	✓	
Cash purchases ▼	295	✓	
Sales ledger control ▼	8,255		✓

Task 8

(a)

Account	Balance b/d at 1 February	Debit	Credit
Loan from bank	53,475		✓
Motor Vehicles	34,900	✓	

Tutorial note.

Loan from bank

Date 20XX	Details	Amount £	Date 20XX	Details	Amount £
15 Jan	Bank	3,050	1 Jan	Balance b/f	36,525
31 Jan	Balance c/d	53,475	31 Jan	Bank	20,000
	Total	56,525		Total	56,525

Motor Vehicles

Date 20XX	Details	Amount £	Date 20XX	Details	Amount £
1 Jan	Balance b/f	32,900	30 Jan	Journal	500
8 Jan	Bank	2,500	31 Jan	Balance c/d	34,900
	Total	35,400		Total	35,400

(b) Trevor Tate

Date 20XX	Details	Amount £	Date 20XX	Details	Amount £
1 Jan	Balance b/f	9,899	22 Jan	Bank	5,780
11 Jan	Invoice 155	1,001	29 Jan	Credit Note C15	714
		▼	31 Jan	Balance c/d ▼	4,406
	Total	10,900		Total	10,900
1 Feb	Balance b/d ▼	4,406		▼	

Task 9

Trial balance as at 31 March

Account name	Amount £	Debit £	Credit £
Sales			91,500
Purchases		34,156	
Administration expenses	8,965	8,965	
Bank (overdraft)	3,000		3,000
Motor vehicle	35,505	35,505	
Motor expenses	1,392	1,392	
Sales ledger control	21,456	21,456	
Purchase ledger control	8,423		8,423
Rent and rates	3,250	3,250	
Capital	1,801		1,801
Totals		104,724	104,724

Task 10

(a)

General plc   Account code: | GENE02 | **Mulitpack Ltd**   Account code: | MULT01 |

(b)

Action	✓
Record the amount paid in the cash book and ledgers.	✓
Change the amounts of the original invoice in the purchases ledger.	
Receive a credit note for the discount taken plus VAT.	✓
Request a new invoice for the amount actually paid.	

(c)

Assets £	Liabilities £	Capital £
149,056	27,446	121,610

Tutorial note.

Assets = £111,000 + £11,433 +£15,390 + £11,233 = £149,056

Liabilities = £5,000 + £22,446 = £27,446

Capital = Assets – Liabilities = £149,056 – £27,446 = £121,610

(d)

Transaction	Classification
Purchased computers for use in the office.	Capital expenditure
Purchased stationery for use in the office.	Revenue expenditure
Purchased a car for the sales person to use for business trips.	Capital expenditure
Received cheque for the sale of goods.	Revenue income
Sold a van the company owned.	Capital income

BPP PRACTICE ASSESSMENT 2
Bookkeeping Transactions

Time allowed: 2 hours

Bookkeeping Transactions
BPP practice assessment 2

Task 1

On 5 July Trappic Ltd delivered the following goods to a credit customer, Nemesis Ltd.

Trappic Ltd	
8 Highview Road Arbuckle AR7 4LX	Nemesis Ltd 36 Ventnor Road Arbuckle AR7 9LC
Delivery note No. 8793 05 July 20XX	Customer account code: NEM893
200 polishing cloths, product code C420.	

The list price of the goods was £0.50 per cloth plus VAT. Nemesis Ltd is to be given a 10% trade discount and a 4% bulk discount.

(a)   Complete the invoice below.

Trappic Ltd

8 Highview Road
Arbuckle
AR7 4LX

Nemesis Ltd
36 Ventnor Road
Arbuckle
AR7 9LC
Date: 6 July 20XX

Invoice No: 67282
Delivery note number: 8793

VAT Registration No. 782 8723 23

Customer account code: NEM893

Quantity of goods	Product code	Total list price £	Net amount after trade discount £	Net amount after all discounts £	VAT £	Gross £

(b) **What will be the amounts entered in the sales daybook when the invoice in (a) has been prepared?**

Sales daybook

Date 20XX	Details	Invoice number	Total £	VAT £	Net £
6 July	Nemesis Ltd	67282			

Trappic Ltd offers each customer a discount of 5% if any order amounts to £1,000 or over.

(c) **What is the name of this type of discount?**

Picklist:

Bulk discount
Prompt payment discount
Trade discount

The account shown below is in the sales ledger of Trappic Ltd. A cheque for £2,311 has now been received from this customer.

Sibley & Co

Date 20XX	Details	Amount £	Date 20XX	Details	Amount £
1 May	Balance b/d	2,897	2 June	Sales returns credit note 5530	173
3 June	Sales invoice 66100	2,556	25 June	Bank	2,724
28 June	Sales Invoice 66800	2,453	26 June	Sales returns credit note 5570	245

(d) Which outstanding item has not been included in the payment of £2,311?

	▼

Picklist:

Balance b/d
Bank
Sales invoice 66100
Sales invoice 66800
Sales returns credit note 5530
Sales returns credit note 5570

Sales invoice 66801 for £4,866.00 including VAT has been sent to Sibley & Co offering a prompt payment discount of 3% for payment within 14 days.

(e) What will be the amount Sibley & Co will pay if they pay within 14 days?

£ [ ]

Task 2

A supply of cleaning fluid has been delivered to Trappic Ltd by OMKG Chemicals. The purchase order sent from Trappic Ltd, and the invoice from OMKG Chemicals, are shown below.

Trappic Ltd
8 Highview Road
Arbuckle
AR7 4LX

Purchase Order No. 637821

To: OMKG Chemicals

Date: 15 July 20XX

Please supply 1000 litres cleaning fluid product code 7638XX
Purchase price: £8.00 per 10 litres, plus VAT
Discount: less 15% trade discount, as agreed

OMKG Chemicals
76 Grange Road, Arbuckle AR1 0HJ
VAT Registration No. 653 9922 33

Invoice No. 76383

Trappic Ltd
8 Highview Road
Arbuckle
AR7 4LX

22 July 20XX

1,000 litres cleaning fluid product code 7638XX @ £0.80 per litre	£800.00
Less trade discount at 12.5%	£100.00
	£700.00
VAT @ 20%	£140.00
Total	£840.00

Terms: 30 days net

(a) **Check the invoice against the purchase order and answer the following questions.**

	Yes ✓	No ✓
Has the correct purchase price of the cleaning fluid been charged?		
Has the correct discount been applied?		
What would be the VAT amount charged if the invoice was correct?	£	
What would be the total amount charged if the invoice was correct?	£	

The credit note below has been received from Bingley & Co in relation to some faulty goods.

Credit note

Bingley & Co
VAT Registration number 436 4472 01

Credit note No. 09374

To: Trappic Ltd   22 July 20XX

	£
1,120 product code XX42 @ £0.50 each	560
VAT @ 20%	112
Total	672

Reason: faulty goods

(b) Record the credit note in the appropriate daybook by:

- **selecting the correct daybook title and**
- **making the necessary entries.**

Picklist:
Discounts allowed daybook
Discounts received daybook
Purchases daybook
Purchases returns daybook
Sales daybook
Sales returns daybook

Date 20XX	Details	Credit note number	Total £	VAT £	Net £
22 Jul	▼	09374			

Picklist:
Bingley & Co
Trappic Ltd

Task 3

Shown below is a statement of account received from a credit supplier, and the supplier's account as shown in the purchases ledger of Trappic Ltd.

<table>
<tr><td colspan="6">Lemonfresh Ltd
90 West Street
Arbuckle
AR4 8AM</td></tr>
<tr><td colspan="6">To: Trappic Ltd
8 Highview Road
Arbuckle
AR7 4LX</td></tr>
<tr><td colspan="6">STATEMENT OF ACCOUNT</td></tr>
</table>

Date 20XX	Invoice Number	Details	Invoice amount £	Cheque amount £	Balance £
1 May	1267	Goods	180		180
3 June	1387	Goods	230		410
7 June	1422	Goods	290		700
10 June	1498	Goods	800		1,500
16 June		Cheque		510	990

Lemonfresh Ltd

Date 20XX	Details	Amount £	Date 20XX	Details	Amount £
16 June	Bank	510	1 May	Purchases	180
16 June	Discount	10	3 June	Purchases	230
			7 June	Purchases	290

(a) **Which item is missing from the statement of account from Lemonfresh Ltd?**

▼

Picklist:

Cheque for £510
Discount for £10
Invoice 1267
Invoice 1387
Invoice 1422
Invoice 1498

(b) Which item is missing from the supplier account in Trappic Ltd's purchases ledger?

	▼

Picklist:

Cheque for £510
Discount for £10
Invoice 1267
Invoice 1387
Invoice 1422
Invoice 1498

(c) Assuming any differences between the statement of account from Lemonfresh Ltd and the supplier account in Trappic Ltd's purchases ledger are simply due to omission errors, what is the amount owing to Lemonfresh Ltd?

£ [ ]

(d) Trappic Ltd prepares a remittance advice note in respect of Lemonfresh Ltd.

Which of the following statements is true?

	✓
The remittance advice note will be sent to the customer to advise them of the amount being paid	
The remittance advice note will be sent to the supplier's bank to advise them of the amount being paid	
The remittance advice note will be sent to the supplier to advise them of the amount being paid	
The remittance advice note will be sent to the accounts department at Lemonfresh Ltd to request that a cheque is raised	

An invoice dated 18 June 20XX has been received from Lemonfresh Ltd for £760.00 plus VAT. A prompt payment discount of 5% is offered for payment within 10 days.

(e) Calculate the amount to be paid to Lemonfresh Ltd if the discount is taken and show the date by which Lemonfresh Ltd should receive the payment.

Supplier	£	Date by which payment should be received by supplier
Lemonfresh Ltd		▼

Picklist:

18 June 20XX
27 June 20XX
28 June 20XX
29 June 20XX
30 June 20XX

Task 4

Russell Hardware has made three payments which are to be entered in its cash book.

Receipts for payments

Received cash with thanks for goods bought. From Russell Hardware, a customer without a credit account. Net £240 VAT £48 Total £288 *Gesteor & Co*	Received cash with thanks for stationery bought. From Russell Hardware, a customer without a credit account. Net £167 (No VAT) *Stationery Shop*

Cheque book stubs

Weston Ltd
(Purchase ledger account WES001)

£1,452

In settlement of outstanding balance
109923

(a) **Enter the details from the payments into the credit side of the cash book shown below and total each column.**

Cash book – credit side

Details	Cash £	Bank £	VAT £	Trade payables £	Cash purchases £	Stationery £
Balance b/f		135				
▽						
▽						
▽						
Totals						

Picklist:

Bank
Cash
Gesteor & Co
Stationery
Stationery Shop
Trade payables
VAT
Weston Ltd

There are also two cheques from credit customers to be entered in Russell Hardware's cash book:

Middle Firth Ltd	£673
High Tops plc	£1,092

(b) **Enter the above details into the debit side of the cash book and total each column.**

Cash book – debit side

Details	Cash £	Bank £	Trade receivables £
Balance b/f	629		
Middle Firth Ltd			
High Tops plc			
Total			

(c) **Using your answers to (a) and (b) above, calculate the cash balance.**

£ [ ]

(d) **Using your answers to (a) and (b) above, calculate the bank balance. Use a minus sign if your calculations indicate an overdrawn bank balance, eg –123.**

£ [ ]

(e) **Will the bank balance calculated in (d) above be a debit or credit balance?**

	✓
Debit	
Credit	

Task 5

This is a summary of petty cash payments made by Russell Hardware.

Office Supplies Ltd paid	£26.00 (plus VAT)
Post Office paid	£12.00 (no VAT)
RN Travel paid	£33.00 (no VAT)

(a) Complete the petty cash book by:

- **Entering the three transactions into the petty cash book below.**

- **Totalling the petty cash book and inserting the balance carried down.**

Petty cash book

Debit side		Credit side					
Details	Amount £	Details	Amount £	VAT £	Postage £	Travel £	Office expenses £
Balance b/f	250.00	▼					
		▼					
		▼					
		▼					
Total		Totals					

Picklist:

Amount
Balance b/d
Balance c/d
Details
Office expenses
Office Supplies Ltd
Post Office
Postage
RN Travel
Travel
VAT

Part way through the month the petty cash account had a balance of £98.40. The cash in the petty cash box was checked and the following notes and coins were there.

Notes and coins	£
3 × £20 notes	60.00
1 × £10 note	10.00
1 × £5 note	5.00
13 × £1 coins	13.00
5 × 50p coins	2.50
21 × 10p coins	2.10
12 × 5p coins	0.60

(b) **Reconcile the cash amount in the petty cash box with the balance on the petty cash account.**

Amount in petty cash box	£	
Balance on petty cash account	£	
Difference	£	

At the end of the month the cash in the petty cash box was £11.95.

(c) **Complete the petty cash reimbursement document below to restore the imprest amount of £250.**

Petty cash reimbursement		
Date: 31.07.20XX		
Amount required to restore the cash in the petty cash box	£	

Task 6

These are the totals of the discounts received daybook at the end of the month.

Discounts received daybook

Details	Total £	VAT £	Net £
Totals	444	74	370

(a) What will be the entries in the general ledger?

Account name	Amount £	Debit ✓	Credit ✓
▼			
▼			
▼			

Picklist:

Discounts allowed
Discounts received
Purchases
Purchases ledger control
Purchases returns
Sales
Sales ledger control
Sales returns
VAT

One of the entries in the discounts received daybook is for a credit note received from Roger Ras for £224 plus VAT.

(b) What will be the entry in the purchases ledger?

Account name	Amount £	Debit ✓	Credit ✓
▼			

Picklist:

Discounts allowed
Discounts received
Purchases
Purchases ledger control
Purchases returns
Roger Ras
Sales
Sales ledger control
Sales returns
VAT

Task 7

The following transactions all took place on 30 June and have been entered into the sales day book as shown below. No entries have yet been made into the ledger system.

Sales day book

Date 20XX	Details	Invoice number	Total £	VAT £	Net £
30 Jun	Trilby & Co	5264	3,936	656	3,280
30 Jun	R Strang Ltd	5265	1,776	296	1,480
	Totals		5,712	952	4,760

(a) What will be the entries in the sales ledger?

Sales ledger

Account name	Amount £	Debit ✓	Credit ✓
▼			
▼			

Picklist:

Purchases
Purchases ledger control
Purchases returns
R Strang Ltd
Sales
Sales ledger control
Sales returns
Trilby & Co
VAT

(b) What will be the entries in the general ledger?

General ledger

Account name	Amount £	Debit ✓	Credit ✓
▼			
▼			
▼			

Picklist:

Purchases
Purchases ledger control
Purchases returns
R Strang Ltd
Sales
Sales ledger control
Sales returns
Trilby & Co
VAT

Task 8

The following two accounts are in the general ledger at the close of day on 30 June.

(a) **Complete the accounts below by:**

- **inserting the balance carried down together with date and details.**
- **inserting the totals.**
- **inserting the balance brought down together with date and details.**

Heat and light

Date 20XX	Details	Amount £	Date 20XX	Details	Amount £
01 Jun	Balance b/d	2,039	▼	▼	
26 Jun	Purchases ledger control	348	▼	▼	
▼		▼	▼	▼	
	Total			Total	
▼		▼	▼	▼	

Picklist:

1 Jul
30 Jun
Balance b/d
Balance c/d
Bank
Purchases ledger control

Sales

Date 20XX	Details		Amount £	Date 20XX	Details		Amount £
		▼		01 Jun	Balance b/d		32,986
		▼		22 Jun	Bank		750
▼		▼		▼		▼	
	Total				Total		
▼		▼		▼		▼	

Picklist:

1 Jul
30 Jun
Balance b/d
Balance c/d
Bank
Sales ledger control

The following account is in the sales ledger at the close of day on 30 June.

Tango Ltd

Date 20XX	Details	Amount £	Date 20XX	Details	Amount £
1 Jun	Balance b/f	899	22 Jun	Bank	780
11 Jun	Invoice 158	201	29 Jun	Credit Note 18	71

(b)   What will be the balance brought down at 1 July on Tango Ltd's account?

Account	Balance b/d at 1 July	Debit ✓	Credit ✓
Tango Ltd			

Task 9

Below are two general ledger accounts and a partially completed trial balance.

Complete the trial balance by:

- transferring the balances of the two general ledger accounts to the debit or credit column of the trial balance.
- entering the amounts shown against each of the other account names into the debit or credit column of the trial balance.
- totalling both columns of the trial balance

Do not enter figures with decimal places in this task and do not enter a zero in unused column cells.

Discounts received

Date 20XX	Details	Amount £	Date 20XX	Details	Amount £
31 Mar			1 Mar	Balance b/f	150
31 Mar	Balance c/d	987	31 Mar	Sales ledger control	837
		987			987

Machinery

Date 20XX	Details	Amount £	Date 20XX	Details	Amount £
1 Mar	Balance b/f	5,300	31 Mar	Balance c/d	15,000
31 Mar	Bank	9,700			
		15,000			15,000

Account name	Amount £	Debit £	Credit £
Discounts received			
Machinery			
Cash at bank	1,342		
Sales ledger control	9,486		
Purchases ledger control	4,003		
VAT (owing to HM Revenue & Customs)	1,880		
Capital	10,000		
Loan from bank	2,500		
Sales	86,262		

Account name	Amount £	Debit £	Credit £
Purchases	43,278		
Administration expenses	1,234		
Totals			

Task 10

Trappic Ltd codes all purchase invoices with a supplier code AND a general ledger code. A selection of the codes used is given below.

Supplier	Supplier Code
Bridgend plc	BRI12
Distinct Ltd	DIS53
Finish Clear & Co	FIN09
Hepplewhite Clean Ltd	HEP76
Mirrors and Glass Ltd	MIR22

Item	General Ledger Code
Cleaning fluids	GL234
Mops and buckets	GL237
Brushes	GL240
Cloths	GL244
Protective clothing	GL248

This is an invoice received from a supplier.

Distinct Ltd **89 Northcourt Road, Arbuckle AR5 3VB** **VAT Registration No. 837 4777 33**	
Trappic Ltd 8 Highview Road Arbuckle AR7 4LX 22 July 20XX	
10 mops with buckets @ £12.60 each	£126.00
VAT @ 20%	£25.20
Total	£151.20

(a) **Select which codes would be used to code this invoice.**

Supplier code	▼
General ledger code	▼

Picklist:

BRI12
DIS53
FIN09
HEP76
MIR22
GL234
GL237
GL240
GL244
GL248

(b) **Why is it necessary to use a supplier code?**

▼

Picklist:

To help find the total amount of purchases
To help trace relevant information quickly and easily
To help when ordering an item
To help when storing an item of inventory

The transactions below have taken place.

(c) **Select one option in each instance below to show whether, in relation to Trappic Ltd, the item will be capital expenditure, revenue expenditure, capital income or revenue income.**

Item	Capital expenditure ✓	Revenue expenditure ✓	Capital income ✓	Revenue income ✓
Purchase of mops and buckets for resale				
Receipt from sale of an item of Trappic Ltd's machinery				
Purchase of delivery vehicle				
Cash purchases of stationery				
Payments to credit suppliers				
Sale of goods for cash				

Financial accounting is based upon the accounting equation.

(d) **Show whether the following statements are True or False.**

	True ✓	False ✓
Income less expenditure is equal to assets		
Capital plus liabilities are equal to assets		
Liabilities equal assets plus capital		

(e) **Classify each of the following items as an asset, a liability or capital.**

Item	Asset, liability or capital?
Money contributed by the owners	▼
Bank overdraft	▼
Petty cash	▼

Picklist:

Asset
Capital
Liability

BPP PRACTICE ASSESSMENT 2
Bookkeeping Transactions

ANSWERS

Bookkeeping Transactions
BPP practice assessment 2

Task 1

(a)

Trappic Ltd
8 Highview Road
Arbuckle
AR7 4LX

VAT Registration No. 782 8723 23

Nemesis Ltd	Customer account code: NEM893
36 Ventnor Road	
Arbuckle	
AR7 9LC	
	Date: 6 July 20XX
Invoice No: 67282	
Delivery note number: 8793	

Quantity of goods	Product code	Total list price £	Net amount after trade discount £	Net amount after all discounts £	VAT £	Gross £
200	C420	100.00	90.00	86.40	17.28	103.68

Tutorial note. The trade discount is deducted first, followed by the bulk discount.

Workings: List price £200 × 0.50 = £100.00, Net after trade discount = £100 × 90% = £90.00, Net after trade and bulk discounts = £90 × 96% = £86.40 VAT = £86.40 × 20% = £17.28

(b) Sales daybook

Date 20XX	Details	Invoice number	Total £	VAT £	Net £
6 July	Nemesis Ltd	67282	103.68	17.28	86.40

(c) The correct answer is: bulk discount

(d) The correct answer is: sales invoice 66800

(e) The correct answer is: £4,720.02

Tutorial note. £4,866.00 × 97% = £4,720.02

Task 2

(a)

	Yes ✓	No ✓
Has the correct purchase price of the cleaning fluid been charged?	✓	
Has the correct discount been applied?		✓
What would be the VAT amount charged if the invoice was correct?	£	136
What would be the total amount charged if the invoice was correct?	£	816

Tutorial note.

VAT: (£800 – (£800 × 15%)) × 20/100 = £136

Total: (£800 – (£800 × 15%)) + £136 = £816

(b) | **Purchases returns daybook** |

Date 20XX	Details	Credit note number	Total £	VAT £	Net £
22 July	Bingley & Co	09374	672	112	560

BPP
LEARNING MEDIA

Task 3

(a) The correct answer is: discount for £10

(b) The correct answer is: invoice 1498

(c) The correct answer is: £980

£990 – £10 = <u>£980</u>

(d) The correct answer is: the remittance advice note will be sent to the supplier to advise them of the amount being paid

(e)

Supplier	£	Date by which payment should be received by supplier
Lemonfresh Ltd	866.40	28 June 20XX

Tutorial note.

Working: VAT = £760 × 20% = £152, Gross amount = £760 + £152 = £912,

Gross less discount = £912 × 95% = £866.40

Task 4

(a) Cash book – credit side

Details	Cash £	Bank £	VAT £	Trade payables £	Cash purchases £	Stationery £
Balance b/f		135				
Gesteor & Co	288		48		240	
Stationery Shop	167					167
Weston Ltd		1,452		1,452		
Totals	455	1,587	48	1,452	240	167

(b)   Cash book – debit side

Details	Cash £	Bank £	Trade receivables £
Balance b/f	629		
Middle Firth Ltd		673	673
High Tops plc		1,092	1,092
Total	629	1,765	1,765

(c)   The correct answer is: £174 (£629 – £455 = £174)

(d)   The correct answer is: £178 (£1,765 – £1,587 = £178)

(e)   The correct answer is: Debit

Task 5

(a) Petty cash book

Debit side		Credit side					
Details	Amount £	Details	Amount £	VAT £	Postage £	Travel £	Office expenses £
Balance b/f	250.00	Office Supplies Ltd	31.20	5.20			26.00
		Post Office	12.00		12.00		
		RN Travel	33.00			33.00	
		Balance c/d	173.80				
	250.00		250.00	5.20	12.00	33.00	26.00

(b)

Amount in petty cash box	£	93.20
Balance on petty cash account	£	98.40
Difference	£	5.20

(c)

Petty cash reimbursement		
Date: 31.07.20XX		
Amount required to restore the cash in the petty cash box	£	238.05

Tutorial note. £250 – £11.95 = £238.05

Task 6

(a)

Account name		Amount £	Debit ✓	Credit ✓
Discounts received	▼	370		✓
VAT	▼	74		✓
Purchases ledger control	▼	444	✓	

(b)

Account name		Amount £	Debit ✓	Credit ✓
Roger Ras	▼	268.80	✓	

Tutorial note. Working VAT: £224 × 20% = £44.80, Gross = £224 + £44.80 = £268.80

· ·

Task 7

(a) Sales ledger

Account name	Amount £	Debit ✓	Credit ✓
Trilby & Co	3,936	✓	
R Strang Ltd	1,776	✓	

(b) General ledger

Account name	Amount £	Debit ✓	Credit ✓
Sales	4,760		✓
VAT	952		✓
Sales ledger control	5,712	✓	

· ·

Task 8

(a)

Heat and light

Date 20XX	Details	Amount £	Date 20XX	Details	Amount £
01 Jun	Balance b/d	2,039			
26 Jun	Purchases ledger control	348	30 Jun	Balance c/d	2,387
	Total	2,387		Total	2,387
1 Jul	Balance b/d	2,387			

Sales

Date 20XX	Details	Amount £	Date 20XX	Details	Amount £
			01 Jun	Balance b/d	32,986
30 Jun	Balance c/d	33,736	22 Jun	Bank	750
	Total	33,736		Total	33,736
			1 Jul	Balance b/d	33,736

(b)

Account	Balance b/d at 1 July	Debit ✓	Credit ✓
Tango Ltd	249	✓	

Tutorial note.

Tango Ltd

Date 20XX	Details	Amount £	Date 20XX	Details	Amount £
1 Jun	Balance b/f	899	22 Jun	Bank	780
11 Jun	Invoice 158	201	29 Jun	Credit Note 18	71
			30 Jun	Balance c/d	249
	Total	1,100		Total	1,100
1 Jul	Balance b/d	249			

Task 9

Account name	Amount £	Debit £	Credit £
Discounts received			987
Machinery		15,000	
Cash at bank	1,342	1,342	
Sales ledger control	9,486	9,486	
Purchases ledger control	4,003		4,003
VAT (owing to HM Revenue & Customs)	1,880		1,880
Capital	4,708		4,708
Loan from bank	2,500		2,500
Sales	86,262		56,262
Purchases	43,278	43,278	
Administration expenses	1,234	1,234	
Totals		70,340	70,340

Task 10

(a)

Supplier code	DIS53
General ledger code	GL237

(b)   The correct answer is: to help trace relevant information quickly and easily

(c)

Item	Capital expenditure ✓	Revenue expenditure ✓	Capital income ✓	Revenue income ✓
Purchase of mops and buckets for resale		✓		
Receipt from sale of an item of Trappic Ltd's machinery			✓	
Purchase of delivery vehicle	✓			
Cash purchases of stationery		✓		
Payments to credit suppliers		✓		
Sale of goods for cash				✓

(d)

	True ✓	False ✓
Income less expenditure is equal to assets		✓
Capital plus liabilities are equal to assets	✓	
Liabilities equal assets plus capital		✓

(e)

Item	Asset, liability or capital?
Money contributed by the owners	Capital
Bank overdraft	Liability
Petty cash	Asset

BPP PRACTICE ASSESSMENT 3
Bookkeeping Transactions

Time allowed: 2 hours

Bookkeeping Transactions
BPP practice assessment 3

Task 1

On 10 July Hazelcombe & Co delivered the following goods to a credit customer, Warriner plc.

Hazelcombe & Co 42 Turnstile Trading Estate Luscombe LU9 0FG Delivery note No. 90230 10 July 20XX Warriner plc   Customer account code: W981 45 Printer Lane Luscombe LU3 9LA 500 fixings, product code FX827.

The list price of the goods was £20.00 per box of 10 fixings plus VAT. Warriner plc is to be given a 20% trade discount.

(a) Calculate the amounts to be included in the invoice.

	£
Net amount before discount	
Net amount after discount	
VAT	
Total	

(b) What will be the amounts entered in the sales daybook when the invoice in (a) has been prepared?

Sales daybook

Date 20XX	Details	Invoice number	Total £	VAT £	Net £
11 Jul	Warriner plc	21026			

The account shown below is in the sales ledger of Hazelcombe & Co. A remittance advice for an automated payment of £3,376 has now been received from this customer.

Oster Ltd

Date 20XX	Details	Amount £	Date 20XX	Details	Amount £
15 May	Sales invoice 19011	1,920	28 May	Sales returns credit note 801	84
16 June	Sales invoice 20332	1,743	15 June	Bank	1,836
17 June	Sales invoice 21276	1,633	15 June	Discount allowed	56
22 June	Sales invoice 21280	650	23 June	Sales returns credit note 893	209

(c) Show which THREE transactions are still outstanding by circling the relevant transactions below.

Transactions
Invoice 19011   Invoice 20332   Invoice 21276   Invoice 21280
Credit note 801   Bank   Discount allowed   Credit note 893

An invoice is being prepared to be sent Oster Ltd for £1,180.00 plus VAT. A prompt payment discount of 2% will be offered for payment within 10 days.

(d) What is the amount Hazelcombe & Co should receive if payment is NOT made within 10 days?

£

(e) What is the amount Hazelcombe & Co should receive if payment is made within 10 days?

£

Task 2

A supply of parts has been delivered to Hazelcombe & Co by Handiparts Ltd. The purchase order sent from Hazelcombe & Co, and the invoice from Handiparts Ltd, are shown below.

Hazelcombe & Co
42 Turnstile Trading Estate
Luscombe
LU9 0FG

Purchase Order No. 89374

To: Handiparts Ltd

Date: 10 July 20XX

Please supply 5000 facings, product code 76253AA
Purchase price: £22.00 per 50, plus VAT
Discount: less 20% trade discount, as agreed

Handiparts Ltd
87 Radley Road, Luscombe LU8 4AZ
VAT Registration No. 874 2309 93

Invoice No. 8749

Hazelcombe & Co
42 Turnstile Trading Estate
Luscombe
LU9 0FG

12 July 20XX

5000 facings product code 7253AA @ £0.50 each	£2,500.00
Less trade discount at 20%	£500.00
Net amount	£2,000.00
VAT @ 20%	£ 400.00
Total	£2,400.00

Terms: 30 days net

(a) **Check the invoice against the purchase order and answer the following questions.**

	Yes ✓	No ✓
Has the correct purchase price of the facings been charged?		
Has the correct discount rate been applied?		
What would be the VAT amount charged if the invoice was correct?	£	
What would be the total amount charged if the invoice was correct?	£	

The credit note below has been received from a credit supplier, Corona Ltd, in respect of a prompt payment discount taken.

Credit note

Corona Ltd	
VAT Registration number 436 4472 01	
Credit note No. 89	
To: Hazelcombe & Co	13 July 20XX
	£
Prompt payment discount taken	66.50
VAT @ 20%	13.30
Total	79.80
Reason: prompt payment discount taken	

(b) **Record the credit note in the appropriate daybook by:**

- **selecting the correct daybook title and**
- **making the necessary entries.**

[▼]

Picklist:

Discounts allowed daybook
Discounts received daybook
Purchases daybook
Purchases returns daybook
Sales daybook
Sales returns daybook

Date 20XX	Details	Credit note number	Total £	VAT £	Net £
13 Jul	▼	89			

Picklist:
Corona Ltd
Hazelcombe & Co

Task 3

Shown below is a statement of account received from a credit supplier, SpareParts plc, and the supplier's account as shown in the purchases ledger of Hazelcombe & Co.

SpareParts plc
Unit 50 Hunston Park Trading Estate
Luscombe
LU3 6XC

To: Hazelcombe & Co
42 Turnstile Trading Estate
Luscombe
LU9 0FG

STATEMENT OF ACCOUNT

Date 20XX	Number	Details	Amount £	Balance £
15 May	I893	Invoice	2,395	2,395
6 June	C043	Credit note	–456	1,939
11 June	I999	Invoice	7,832	9,771
17 June	I034	Invoice	2,347	12,118
30 June		Payment	–2,395	9,723

SpareParts plc

Date 20XX	Details	Amount £	Date 20XX	Details	Amount £
29 June	Bank – cheque	2,395	15 May	Purchases	2,395
29 June	Discount	27	11 June	Purchases	7,832
			17 June	Purchases	2,347

(a) Which item is missing from the statement of account from SpareParts plc?

	▼

Picklist:

Cheque for £2,395
Credit note C043
Discount for £27
Invoice I034
Invoice I893
Invoice I999

(b) Which item is missing from the supplier account in Hazelcombe & Co's purchases ledger?

	▼

Picklist:

Cheque for £2,395
Credit note C043
Discount for £27
Invoice I034
Invoice I893
Invoice I999

(c) Assuming any differences between the statement of account from SpareParts plc and the supplier account in Hazelcombe & Co's purchases ledger are simply due to omission errors, what is the amount owing to SpareParts plc?

£ [   ]

This is the account of Cooper Foundry Ltd in the purchases ledger of Hazelcombe & Co, and an invoice that has been received from the supplier but not yet entered into their account.

Cooper Foundry Ltd

Date 20XX	Details	Amount £	Date 20XX	Details	Amount £
1 July	Bank	2,450	1 July	Balance b/f	3,235
1 July	Discount received	80	1 July	Invoice 09364	982
6 July	Credit note 039	45	15 July	Invoice 09528	2,386

Invoice

```
                Cooper Foundry Ltd
     VAT Registration number 896 5421 01

              Invoice No. 6532

To: Hazelcombe & Co        20 July 20XX
                                    £
Goods supplied 100 product
C456                               275
VAT @ 20%                           55
Total                              330

          Terms: net monthly account
```

(d) What will be the amount to be paid to Cooper Foundry Ltd once the invoice has been entered into their account?

£ ▢

The two invoices below were received on 20 July from credit suppliers who offer a prompt payment discount.

Invoice

```
                 Brixton Ltd
     VAT Registration number 569 4453 01

              Invoice No. 9932

To: Hazelcombe & Co        20 July 20XX
                                    £
Goods supplied                  2,500
VAT @ 20%                         500
Total                           3,000

  Terms: 4% discount if payment received
     within 10 days of date of invoice.
```

Invoice

```
                 Harrier Ltd
     VAT Registration number 442 6753 00

              Invoice No. H321

To: Hazelcombe & Co        20 July 20XX
                                    £
Goods supplied                    595
VAT @ 20%                         119
Total                             714

  Terms: 2% discount if payment received
     within 14 days of date of invoice.
```

(e) Calculate the amount to be paid to each supplier if the discount is taken and show the date by which the supplier should receive the payment.

Supplier	£	Date by which payment should be received by supplier
Brixton Ltd		▼
Harrier Ltd		▼

Picklist:

20 July
30 July
31 July
3 August
4 August

Task 4

Finn Clothing has made two payments which are to be entered in its cash book.

Receipts for payment

Received cash with thanks for goods bought.

From Finn Clothing, a customer without a credit account.

Net   £920
VAT   £184
Total   £1,104

Wisper & Co

Cheque book stub

Lampetus Ltd
(Purchases ledger account LAM001)

£2,135
In settlement of outstanding account

003456

(a) **Make the necessary entries in the cash book and total each column. Cash book – credit side**

Details	Cash £	Bank £	VAT £	Trade payables £	Cash purchases £
Balance b/f		1,902			
▼					
▼					
Totals					

Picklist:

Bank
Cash purchases
Lampetus Ltd
Trade payables
VAT
Wisper & Co

There are also two cheques from credit customers to be entered in Finn Clothing's cash book:

Prickles & Co   £2,837

Dreston Proops   £3,299

(b) Enter the above details into the debit side of the cash book and total each column.

Cash book – debit side

Details	Cash £	Bank £	Trade receivables £
Balance b/f	1,593		
Prickles & Co			
Dreston Proops			
Total			

(c) Using your answers to (a) and (b) above, calculate the cash balance.

£ [   ]

(d) Using your answers to (a) and (b) above, calculate the bank balance. Use a minus sign if your calculations indicate an overdrawn bank balance, eg –123.

£ [   ]

(e) Will the bank balance calculated in (d) above be a debit or credit balance?

	✓
Debit	
Credit	

Task 5

This is a summary of petty cash payments made by Finn Clothing.

Quick Bus Company paid   £12.50 (no VAT) on 27 September

Star's Stationery paid   £18.00 (plus VAT) on 30 September

Post Office paid   £8.00 (no VAT) on 30 September

(a) **Complete the petty cash book by:**

  • **Entering all the transactions into the petty cash book below.**

  • **Totalling the petty cash book and inserting the balance carried down at 30 September.**

Petty cash book

Date	Details	Amount £	Date	Details	Amount £	VAT £	Stationery £	Travel £	Postage £
23 Sept	Balance b/f	120.00	27 Sept	▼					
			30 Sept	▼					
			30 Sept	▼					
			30 Sept	▼					
	Total			Totals					

Picklist:

Amount
Balance b/d
Balance c/d
Details
Postage
Post Office
Stationery
Star's Stationery
Quick Bus Company
Travel
VAT

(b) **What will be the amount of cash withdrawn from the bank to restore the imprest level of £120.00?**

£ [   ]

Task 6

These are the totals of Hazelcombe & Co's discounts allowed daybook at the end of the month.

Discounts allowed daybook

Details	Total £	VAT £	Net £
Totals	90	15	75

(a) **Post the amounts from the daybook to the general ledger accounts below. You do NOT need to balance off the accounts.**

Discounts allowed

Details		£	Details		£
	▼			▼	
	▼			▼	

Picklist:

Discounts allowed
Discounts received
Purchases
Purchases ledger control
Purchases returns
Sales
Sales ledger control
Sales returns
VAT

VAT

Details		£	Details		£
	▼			▼	
	▼			▼	

Picklist:

Discounts allowed
Discounts received
Purchases
Purchases ledger control
Purchases returns
Sales
Sales ledger control
Sales returns
VAT

Sales ledger control

Details		£	Details		£
	▼			▼	
	▼			▼	

Picklist:

Discounts allowed
Discounts received
Purchases
Purchases ledger control
Purchases returns
Sales
Sales ledger control
Sales returns
VAT

One of the entries in the discounts allowed daybook is for a credit note sent to Susan Smith for £66 plus VAT.

(b) Record the invoice in the appropriate sales ledger account:

- **Selecting the correct sales ledger account and**
- **Making the necessary entries**.

	▼

Picklist:

Discounts allowed
Discounts received
Hazelcombe & Co
Sales
Sales ledger control
Susan Smith

Details		£	Details		£
	▼			▼	
	▼			▼	

Picklist:

Discount allowed
Hazelcombe & Co
Sale
Susan Smith
VAT

Task 7

Hazelcombe & Co maintains a petty cash book as a book of prime entry only. The following transactions all took place on 30 June and have been entered in the petty cash book as shown below. No entries have yet been made in the general ledger.

Petty cash book – credit side

Date 20XX	Details	Amount £	VAT £	Distribution expenses £	Travel £	Office expenses £
30 Jun	Envelopes	18.24	3.04			15.20
30 Jun	Postage	13.40				13.40
30 Jun	De-icer	6.72	1.12	5.60		
30 Jun	Bus fares	17.65			17.65	
		56.01	4.16	5.60	17.65	28.60

What will be the five entries in the general ledger?

General ledger

Account name	Amount £	Debit ✓	Credit ✓
▼			
▼			
▼			
▼			
▼			

Picklist:

Bank
Bus fares
De-icer
Distribution expenses
Envelopes
Office expenses
Petty cash control
Postage
Travel
VAT

Task 8

The following account is in the general ledger at close of day on 30 June.

Purchases

Date 20XX	Details	Amount £	Date 20XX	Details	Amount £
1 Jun	Balance b/f	3,920	30 Jun	Journal	200
8 Jun	Purchases ledger control	2,357			

(a) What will be the balance brought down at 1 July?

Account	Balance b/d at 1 July	Debit ✓	Credit ✓
Purchases			

The following two accounts are in the general ledger and the purchases ledger respectively at the close of day on 30 June.

(b) Complete the accounts below by:

- **Inserting the balance carried down together with date and details.**
- **Inserting the totals.**
- **Inserting the balance brought down together with date and details.**

General ledger

Office expenses

Date 20XX	Details	Amount £	Date 20XX	Details	Amount £
01 Jun	Balance b/d	12,945		▼	
30 Jun	Petty cash	42		▼	
30 Jun	Purchases ledger control	523		▼	
▼	▼		▼	▼	
	Total			Total	
▼	▼		▼	▼	

Picklist:
1 Jul
30 Jun
Balance b/d
Balance c/d
Bank
Petty cash
Purchases ledger control

Purchases ledger

Knowsley & Sons

Date 20XX	Details	Amount £	Date 20XX	Details	Amount £
27 June	Bank	1,009	01 Jun	Balance b/d	1,276
27 June	Discount received	65	16 Jun	Purchases	565
▼	▼		▼	▼	
	Total			Total	
▼	▼		▼	▼	

Picklist:

1 Jul
30 Jun
Balance b/d
Balance c/d
Knowsley & Sons

Task 9

Below are two general ledger accounts and a partially completed trial balance.

Complete the trial balance by:

- **Transferring the balances of the two general ledger accounts to the debit or credit column of the trial balance.**

- **Entering the amounts shown against each of the other account names into the debit or credit column of the trial balance.**

- **Totalling both columns of the trial balance**

Do not enter figures with decimal places in this task and do not enter a zero in unused column cells.

Bank

Date 20XX	Details	Amount £	Date 20XX	Details	Amount £
15 May	Sales ledger control	19,502	1 May	Balance b/f	1,200
31 May	Balance c/d	2,137	25 May	Purchases ledger control	20,439
		21,639			21,639

Purchases

Date 20XX	Details	Amount £	Date 20XX	Details	Amount £
1 May	Balance b/f	58,950	31 May	Balance c/d	81,744
30 May	Purchases ledger control	22,794			
		81,744			81,744

Account name	Amount £	Debit £	Credit £
Bank			
Purchases			
Administrative expenses	52,165		
Capital	4,870		
Discounts allowed	1,986		
Discounts received	2,543		
Inventory	12,354		
Petty cash	250		
Purchases ledger control	6,297		
Sales	152,242		
Sales ledger control	24,910		
VAT (owing to HM Revenue & Customs)	5,320		
Totals			

Task 10

Hazelcombe & Co codes all purchase invoices with a supplier code AND a general ledger code. A selection of the codes used is given below.

Supplier	Supplier Code
Curran Mews Ltd	C783
Findlay & Co	F920
Gosling Ltd	G224
Meston plc	M029
Postlethwaite Brothers	P673

Item	General Ledger Code
Facings	GL956
Fixings	GL962
Leads	GL967
Lights	GL971
Pumps	GL975

This is an invoice received from a supplier.

Findlay & Co
98 Green Road, Luscombe LU9 0CV
VAT Registration No. 987 3666 237

Hazelcombe & Co
42 Turnstile Trading Estate
Luscombe
LU9 0FG

17 July 20XX

20 lights (product code 72836) @ £6.80 each	£136.00
VAT @ 20%	£27.20
Total	£163.20

(a) **Select which codes would be used to code this invoice.**

Supplier code	▼
General ledger code	▼

Picklist:

C783
F920
G224
GL956
GL962
GL967
GL971
GL975
M029
P673

(b) **Why is it necessary to use a general ledger code for different types of purchases?**

	▼

Picklist:

To help find the total amount of purchases
To help identify how much is owed to a supplier
To help identify the amount spent on a particular category of inventory
To help identify when to re-order an item of inventory

(c) **Select one option in each instance below to show whether the item will be capital expenditure, revenue expenditure, capital income or revenue income.**

Item	Capital expenditure ✓	Revenue expenditure ✓	Capital income ✓	Revenue income ✓
Cash sales				
Purchase on credit of lights for resale				
Sale of goods on credit				
Purchase of office computer				
Payments to credit suppliers				
Receipt from sale of an item of Hazelcombe & Co's furniture and fittings				

(d) **Show whether the following statements are True or False.**

	True ✓	False ✓
An increase in an asset is shown as a credit entry in the general ledger		
A decrease in liabilities is shown as a credit entry in the general ledger		
An increase in capital is shown as a credit entry in the general ledger		

(e) **Identify from the picklist an example of an asset, a liability and a capital transaction.**

Item	Example from picklist	
Asset		▼
Liability		▼
Capital transaction		▼

Picklist:

Bank overdraft
Drawings
Trade receivables

BPP PRACTICE ASSESSMENT 3
Bookkeeping Transactions

ANSWERS

Bookkeeping Transactions
BPP practice assessment 3

Task 1

(a)

	£
Net amount before discount	1,000.00
Net amount after discount	800.00
VAT	160.00
Total	960.00

Tutorial note. Working: List price £20 × 500/10 = £1,000, Net after trade discount = £1,000 × 80% = £800, VAT £800 × 20% = £160

(b)   Sales daybook

Date 20XX	Details	Invoice number	Total £	VAT £	Net £
11 Jul	Warriner plc	21026	960.00	160.00	800.00

(c)

Transactions
Invoice 19011   Invoice 20332   Invoice 21276   ⟨Invoice 21280⟩
Credit note 801   Bank   ⟨Discount allowed⟩   ⟨Credit note 893⟩

(d)   The correct answer is: £1,416

Tutorial note.

Working: VAT £1,180 × 20% = £236, Gross £1,180 + £236 = £1,416

(e)   The correct answer is: £1,387.68

Tutorial note.

Working: £1,416 × 98% = £1,387.68

Task 2

(a)

	Yes ✓	No ✓
Has the correct purchase price of the facings been charged?		✓
Has the correct discount rate been applied?	✓	
What would be the VAT amount charged if the invoice was correct?	£	352
What would be the total amount charged if the invoice was correct?	£	2,112

Tutorial note.

VAT: ((5,000 × £22/50) – (5,000 × £22/50 × 20/100)) × 20/100 = £352

Total: (5,000 × £22/50) × 0.80 × 1.2 = £2,112

(b) | Discounts received daybook ▼ |

Date 20XX	Details	Credit note number	Total £	VAT £	Net £
13 Jul	Corona Ltd	89	79.80	13.30	66.50

Task 3

(a) The correct answer is: discount for £27

(b) The correct answer is: credit note C043

(c) The correct answer is: £9,696

Tutorial note. Working: £9,723 – £27 = £9,696

(d) The correct answer is: £4,358

Tutorial note.

Working: £3,235 + £982 + £2,386 – £2,450 – £80 – £45 + £330 = £4,358

(e)

Supplier	£	Date by which payment should be received by supplier
Brixton Ltd	2,880.00	30 July
Harrier Ltd	699.72	3 August

Tutorial note.

Brixton Ltd £3,000 × 96% = £2,880
Harrier Ltd £714 × 98% = £699.72

Task 4

(a) Cash book – credit side

Details	Cash £	Bank £	VAT £	Trade payables £	Cash purchases £
Balance b/f		1,902			
Wisper & Co	1,104		184		920
Lampetus Ltd		2,135		2,135	
Total	1,104	4,037	184	2,135	920

(b) Cash book – debit side

Details	Cash £	Bank £	Trade receivables £
Balance b/f	1,593		
Prickles & Co		2,837	2,837
Dreston Proops		3,299	3,299
Total	1,593	6,136	6,136

(c) The correct answer is: £489 (£1,593 – £1,104 = £489)

(d) The correct answer is: £2,099 (£6,136 – £4,037 = £2,099)

(e) The correct answer is: Debit

Task 5

(a) Petty cash book

Date	Details	Amount £	Date	Details	Amount £	VAT £	Stationery £	Travel £	Postage £
23 Sept	Balance b/f	120.00	27 Sept	Quick Bus Company	12.50			12.50	
			30 Sept	Star's Stationery	21.60	3.60	18.00		
			30 Sept	Post Office	8.00				8.00
			30 Sept	Balance c/d	77.90				
	Total	120.00		Totals	120.00	3.60	18.00	12.50	8.00

(b) The correct answer is: £42.10

Tutorial note. Working: £12.50 + £21.60 + £8.00 = £42.10

Task 6

(a)

Discounts allowed

Details	£	Details	£
Sales ledger control	75		

VAT

Details	£	Details	£
Sales ledger control	15		

Sales ledger control

Details	£	Details	£
		Discounts allowed	75
		VAT	15

(b)

Susan Smith	▼

Details	£	Details	£
		Discount allowed	79.20

Tutorial note. Working VAT = £66 × 20% = £13.20, gross amount = £66 + 13.20 = £79.20

Task 7

General ledger

Account name	Amount £	Debit ✓	Credit ✓
Petty cash control	56.01		✓
Distribution expenses	5.60	✓	
Office expenses	28.60	✓	
Travel	17.65	✓	
VAT	4.16	✓	

Task 8

(a)

Account	Balance b/d at 1 July	Debit ✓	Credit ✓
Purchases	6,077	✓	

Tutorial note.

Purchases

Date 20XX	Details	Amount £	Date 20XX	Details	Amount £
1 Jun	Balance b/f	3,920	30 Jun	Journal	200
8 Jun	Purchases ledger control	2,357	30 Jun	Balance c/d	6,077
	Total	6,277		Total	6,277

(b) General ledger

Office expenses

Date 20XX	Details	Amount £	Date 20XX	Details	Amount £
01 Jun	Balance b/d	12,945			
30 Jun	Petty cash	42			
30 Jun	Purchases ledger control	523	30 Jun	Balance c/d	13,510
	Total	13,510		Total	13,510
1 Jul	Balance b/d	13,510			

Purchases ledger

Knowsley & Sons

Date 20XX	Details	Amount £	Date 20XX	Details	Amount £
27 June	Bank	1,009	01 Jun	Balance b/d	1,276
27 June	Discount received	65	16 Jun	Purchases	565
30 Jun	Balance c/d	767			
	Total	1,841		Total	1,841
			1 Jul	Balance b/d	767

Task 9

Account name	Amount £	Debit £	Credit £
Bank			2,137
Purchases		81,744	
Administrative expenses	52,165	52,165	
Capital	4,870		4,870
Discounts allowed	1,986	1,986	
Discounts received	2,543		2,543
Inventory	12,354	12,354	
Petty cash	250	250	
Purchases ledger control	6,297		6,297
Sales	152,242		152,242
Sales ledger control	24,910	24,910	
VAT (owing to HM Revenue & Customs)	5,320		5,320
Totals		173,409	173,409

Task 10

(a)

Supplier code	F920
General ledger code	GL971

(b) The correct answer is: to help identify the amount spent on a particular category of inventory

(c)

Item	Capital expenditure ✓	Revenue expenditure ✓	Capital income ✓	Revenue income ✓
Cash sales				✓
Purchase on credit of lights for resale		✓		
Sale of goods on credit				✓
Purchase of office computer	✓			

Item	Capital expenditure ✓	Revenue expenditure ✓	Capital income ✓	Revenue income ✓
Payments to credit suppliers		✓		
Receipt from sale of an item of Hazelcombe & Co's furniture and fittings			✓	

(d)

	True ✓	False ✓
An increase in an asset is shown as a credit entry in the general ledger		✓
A decrease in liabilities is shown as a credit entry in the general ledger		✓
An increase in capital is shown as a credit entry in the general ledger	✓	

(e)

Item	Example
Asset	Trade receivables
Liability	Bank overdraft
Capital transaction	Drawings

BPP PRACTICE ASSESSMENT 4
Bookkeeping Transactions

Time allowed: 2 hours

Bookkeeping Transactions
BPP practice assessment 4

Task 1

On 21 July Mandarin Ltd received the following goods returned note from a credit customer, Jessop Brothers.

Jessop Brothers
Unit 10 Eastern Trading Estate
Cinnadon
CN1 1PP

GOODS RETURNED NOTE

GRN no: 567

To: Mandarin Ltd
Mandarin House
25 Jedward Street
Cinnadon
CN6 6LW

21 July 20XX
Delivery note No. 452634

Order No. 876238

20 womens decorative tops, product code WT555.

Reason for return: faulty

The list price of the goods was £30 per box of five tops plus VAT. Jessop Brothers was given a 10% trade discount.

(a) Complete the credit note below.

Mandarin Ltd
Mandarin House, 25 Jedward Street
Cinnadon
CN6 6LW

Jessop Brothers
Unit 10 Eastern Trading Estate
Cinnadon
CN1 1PP
Customer account code: SL930

VAT Registration No. 928 2781 110

CREDIT NOTE

Credit note number no: CN01256
Delivery note number: 452634
Order number: 876238

Date: 22 July 20XX

Quantity of goods	Product code	Total list price £	Net amount after discount £	VAT £	Gross £

(b) **Record the credit note in the appropriate daybook by:**
- **Selecting the correct daybook title and**
- **Making the necessary entries.**

Picklist:

Discounts allowed daybook
Discounts received daybook
Purchases daybook
Purchases returns daybook
Sales daybook
Sales returns daybook

Date 20XX	Details	Credit note number	Total £	VAT £	Net £
22 Jul	▼	CN01256			

Picklist:

Jessop Brothers
Mandarin Ltd

The following is a summary of transactions with Tarsus & Co, a new credit customer.

£324 re invoice 01250 of 21 July
£12 re credit note 013 of 22 July
£1,285 re invoice 01301 of 30 July
Cheque for £302 received 31 July
Prompt payment discount £10 taken 31 July

(c) **Complete the statement of account below by:**
- **Dragging and dropping the dates and details below into the first column**
- **Entering the outstanding amount after every transaction into the final column**

Mandarin Ltd
Mandarin House
25 Jedward Street
Cinnadon
CN6 6LW

To: Tarsus & Co   Date: 31 July 20XX

Date 20XX and details	Transaction amount £	Outstanding amount £
	324	
	12	
	1,285	
	302	
	10	

Date 20XX and details:

21 July – Invoice 01250	22 July – Credit note 013	30 July – Invoice 01301
31 July – Cheque	31 July – Discount taken	

The account shown below is in the sales ledger of Mandarin Ltd. A remittance advice for an automated payment of £1,565 has now been received from this customer.

Plews & Co

Date 20XX	Details	Amount £	Date 20XX	Details	Amount £
12 May	Sales invoice 0024	2,910	15 May	Sales returns credit note 001	125
23 June	Sales invoice 0095	1,663	25 June	Sales returns credit note 017	98
2 July	Sales invoice 0102	2,739	30 June	Bank	2,785

(d) Which outstanding item has not been included in the payment of £1,565?

▼

Picklist:

Bank
Sales invoice 0024
Sales invoice 0095
Sales invoice 0102
Sales returns credit note 001
Sales returns credit note 017

An invoice is being prepared to be sent to Plews & Co for £2,560.00 plus VAT. A prompt payment discount of 5% will be offered for payment within 10 days.

(e) What is the amount Mandarin Ltd should receive if payment is made within 10 days?

£ [   ]

....

Task 2

A supply of clothing has been delivered to Mandarin Ltd by Rainbow Fashions Ltd. The purchase order sent from Mandarin Ltd, and the invoice from Rainbow Fashions Ltd, are shown below.

Mandarin Ltd
Mandarin House, 25 Jedward Street
Cinnadon
CN6 6LW

Purchase Order No. 093247

To: Rainbow Fashions Ltd

Date: 17 July 20XX

Please supply 40 mens polo shirts, product code MPS45
Purchase price: £36.00 per pack of 5, plus VAT
Discount: less 10% trade discount, as agreed
Terms: 2% discount for payment within 14 days

Rainbow Fashions Ltd
92 Norman Street, Cinnadon CN4 2KJ
VAT Registration No. 903 2838 39

Invoice No. 83792

Mandarin Ltd
Mandarin House, 25 Jedward Street
Cinnadon
CN6 6LW

22 July 20XX

40 mens polo shirts product code MPS45 @ £7.60 each	£304.00
Less trade discount at 10%	£30.40
Net amount	£273.60

Terms: 30 days net

(a) **Identify any discrepancies on the invoice by drawing a line from each left hand box to the appropriate right hand box.**

Terms of payment	Not shown on invoice
VAT rate	Incorrectly shown on invoice
Trade discount	
Purchase price	Correctly shown on invoice

(b)

	Yes ✓	No ✓
What would be the VAT amount charged if the invoice was correct?	£	
What would be the total amount charged if the invoice was correct?	£	

Invoices from suppliers have been checked and partially entered in the purchases day book, as shown below.

(c) **Complete the purchases day book by:**

- **Inserting the appropriate figures for each invoice in the relevant columns.**
- **Totalling the last five columns of the purchases day book.**

Purchases day book

Date 20XX	Details	Invoice number	Total £	VAT £	Net £	Women's clothing £	Men's clothing £
30 Jun	Forfar Textiles plc	C9230	1,872				1,560
30 Jun	Jessamy Fashion Inc	0024567	3,216		2,680	2,680	
30 Jun	Lindstrom Ltd	726		648		3,240	
	Totals						

Task 3

Shown below is a statement of account received from a credit supplier, and the supplier's account as shown in the purchases ledger of Mandarin Ltd.

Bella Designs
34-36 Bath Street
Cinnadon
CN3 1GH

To: Mandarin Ltd
Mandarin House
25 Jedward Street
Cinnadon
CN6 6LW

STATEMENT OF ACCOUNT

Date 20XX	Number	Details	Amount £	Balance £
26 May	6723	Invoice	1,092	1,092
3 June	6801	Invoice	894	1,986
15 June		Payment	−1,986	0
15 June	7013	Invoice	3,267	3,267
18 June	C67	Credit note	−62	3,205
27 Jun	7226	Invoice	2,674	5,879
30 June	C98	Credit note	−89	5,790

Bella Designs

Date 20XX	Details	Amount £	Date 20XX	Details	Amount £
15 June	Bank – cheque	1,986	26 May	Purchases	1,092
18 June	Purchases returns	62	3 June	Purchases	894
30 June	Bank – cheque	3,205	15 June	Purchases	3,267
			27 June	Purchases	2,674

(a) **Which item is missing from the statement of account from Bella Designs?**

▼

Picklist:

Credit note C67
Credit note C98
Invoice 6723
Invoice 6801
Invoice 7013
Invoice 7226
Payment for £1,986
Payment for £3,205

(b) **Which item is missing from the supplier account in Mandarin Ltd's purchases ledger?**

▼

Picklist:

Credit note C67
Credit note C98
Invoice 6723
Invoice 6801
Invoice 7013
Invoice 7226
Payment for £1,986
Payment for £3,205

(c) **Assuming any differences between the statement of account from Bella Designs and the supplier account in Mandarin Ltd's purchases ledger are simply due to omission errors, what is the amount owing to Bella Designs?**

£ [   ]

The two invoices below were received on 30 June from credit suppliers who offer a prompt payment discount.

Invoice

Bumble plc	
VAT Registration number 445 5693 01	
Invoice No. F196	
To: Mandarin Ltd	29 June 20XX
	£
150 Leather jackets	3,750.00
VAT @ 20%	750.00
Total	4,500.00

Terms: 1% discount if payment received within 14 days of date of invoice.

Invoice

Hallidays Ltd	
VAT Registration number 675 4423 00	
Invoice No. 658	
To: Mandarin Ltd	29 June 20XX
	£
500 Leather trousers	2,500.00
VAT @ 20%	500.00
Total	3,000.00

Terms: 5% discount if payment received within 10 days of date of invoice.

(d) **Calculate the amount to be paid to each supplier if the discount is taken and show the date by which the supplier should receive the payment.**

Supplier	£	Date by which payment should be received by supplier
Bumble plc		▼
Hallidays Ltd		▼

Picklist:

29 June 20XX
8 July 20XX
9 July 20XX
10 July 20XX
13 July 20XX
14 July 20XX

....

Task 4

The two amounts shown below have been received from customers and are ready to be entered in the cash book.

Vampeter Ltd	Sales receipt
Remittance advice note	15 July 20XX
15 July 20XX Please find enclosed a cheque for £1,256 in settlement of invoice number 4876	£900 including VAT cash received from Propos Co for goods purchased.

(a) **Enter the above details into the debit side of the cash book and total each column.**

Cash book – debit side

Details	Cash £	Bank £	VAT £	Trade receivables £	Cash sales £
Balance b/f	1,869				
Vampeter Ltd					
Propos Co					
Total					

There were also two payments to enter in to the Cash book – credit side.

Cheque book stubs

Diston Ltd (Purchases ledger account DIS057) £4,295 In settlement of outstanding balance 209345	Opra Office Supplies (We have no credit account with this supplier) £336 including VAT 209346

(b) **Enter the details from the payments into the credit side of the cash book shown below and total each column.**

Cash book – credit side

Details	Cash £	Bank £	VAT £	Trade payables £	Cash purchases £	Office expenses £
Balance b/f		1,249				
Diston Ltd						
Opra Office Supplies						
Total						

(c) **Using your answers to (a) and (b) above, calculate the cash balance.**

£

(d) **Using your answers to (a) and (b) above, calculate the bank balance. Use a minus sign if your calculations indicate an overdrawn bank balance, eg –123.**

£

(e) **Will the bank balance calculated in (d) above be a debit or credit balance?**

	✓
Debit	
Credit	

Task 5

This is a summary of petty cash payments made by Scriven Trading.

Harry's Café paid	£26.30 (no VAT)
Tune Travel paid	£32.40 (plus VAT)

(a) Complete the petty cash book by:

- **Entering both transactions into the petty cash book below.**
- **Totalling the petty cash book and inserting the balance carried down.**

Petty cash book

Details	Amount £	Details	Amount £	VAT £	Entertainment £	Travel £
Balance b/f	100.00	▼				
		▼				
		▼				
Total		Totals				

Picklist:

Amount
Balance b/d
Balance c/d
Details
Entertainment
Harry's Café
Travel
Tune Travel
VAT

Mandarin Ltd maintains a petty cash book as a book of prime entry only. The following transactions all took place on 30 June and have been entered in the petty cash book (credit side) as shown below. No entries have yet been made in the general ledger.

Petty cash book – credit side

Date 20XX	Details	Amount £	VAT £	Motor expenses £	Postage £	Sundry expenses £
30 Jun	Taxi fares	15.98				15.98
30 Jun	Printer paper	8.16	1.36			6.80
30 Jun	Petrol	51.36	8.56	42.80		
30 Jun	Postage stamps	17.26			17.26	
		92.76	9.92	42.80	17.26	22.78

(b) What will be the five entries in the general ledger?

General ledger

Account name		Amount £	Debit ✓	Credit ✓
	▼			
	▼			
	▼			
	▼			
	▼			

Picklist:

Bank
Motor expenses
Sundry expenses
Petrol
Petty cash control
Postage
Postage stamps
Printer paper
Taxi fares
VAT

....

Task 6

One of the entries in Mandarin Ltd's discounts allowed daybook is for a credit note sent to Rupert Reynolds for £33 including VAT.

(a) Record the invoice in the appropriate sales ledger account by:

- **selecting the correct sales ledger account and**
- **making the necessary entries.**

	▼

Picklist:

Discounts allowed
Discounts received
Mandarin Ltd
Rupert Reynolds
Sales
Sales ledger control

Details		£	Details		£
	▼			▼	
	▼			▼	

Picklist:

Discount allowed
Mandarin Ltd
Rupert Reynolds
Sale
VAT

These are the totals of Mandarin Ltd's discounts received daybook at the end of the month.

Discounts received daybook

Details	Total £	VAT £	Net £
Totals	762	127	635

(b) **Post the amounts from the daybook to the general ledger accounts below. You do not need to balance off the accounts.**

Discounts received

Details		£	Details		£
	▼			▼	
	▼			▼	

Picklist:

Discounts allowed
Discounts received
Purchases
Purchases ledger control
Purchases returns
Sales
Sales ledger control
Sales returns
VAT

VAT

Details		£	Details		£
	▼			▼	
	▼			▼	

Picklist:

Discounts allowed
Discounts received
Purchases
Purchases ledger control
Purchases returns
Sales
Sales ledger control
Sales returns
VAT

Purchases ledger control

Details		£	Details		£
	▼			▼	
	▼			▼	

Picklist:

Discounts allowed
Discounts received
Purchases
Purchases ledger control
Purchases returns
Sales
Sales ledger control
Sales returns
VAT

Task 7

The following transactions all took place on 30 June and have been entered in the debit side of the cash book as shown below. No entries have yet been made in the ledgers.

Cash book – debit side

Date 20XX	Details	Cash £	Bank £	VAT £	Trade receivables £	Cash sales £
30 Jun	Singer & Co		1,934		1,934	
30 Jun	Cash sale	756		126		630

(a)   What will be the entry in the sales ledger?

Sales ledger

Account name	Amount £	Debit ✓	Credit ✓
▼			

Picklist:

Bank
Cash
Cash sales
Discounts allowed
Discounts received
Purchases
Purchases ledger control
Sales
Sales ledger control
Singer & Co
VAT

(b)   What will be the THREE entries in the general ledger?

General ledger

Account name	Amount £	Debit ✓	Credit ✓
▼			
▼			
▼			

Picklist:

Bank
Cash
Cash sales
Discounts allowed
Discounts received
Purchases
Purchases ledger control
Sales
Sales ledger control
Singer & Co
VAT

Task 8

The following two accounts are in the general ledger at the close of day on 30 June.

(a) Complete the accounts below by:

- **Inserting the balance carried down together with date and details.**
- **Inserting the totals.**
- **Inserting the balance brought down together with date and details.**

Motor expenses

Date 20XX	Details	Amount £	Date 20XX	Details	Amount £
01 Jun	Balance b/d	2,904			
15 Jun	Purchases ledger control	276			
30 Jun	Purchases ledger control	184			
▼		▼	▼		▼
	Total			Total	
▼		▼	▼		▼

Picklist:

1 Jul
30 Jun
Balance b/d
Balance c/d
Bank
Purchases ledger control
Sales ledger control

Discounts received

Date 20XX	Details	Amount £	Date 20XX	Details	Amoun £
			01 Jun	Balance b/d	92€
			15 Jun	Purchases ledger control	6
			30 Jun	Purchases ledger control	2!
▼		▼	▼		▼
	Total			Total	
▼		▼	▼		▼

Picklist:

1 Jul
30 Jun
Balance b/d
Balance c/d
Bank
Purchases ledger control
Sales ledger control

Task 9

Below are two general ledger accounts and a partially completed trial balance.

Complete the trial balance by:

- **Transferring the balances of the two general ledger accounts to the debit or credit column of the trial balance.**
- **Entering the amounts shown against each of the other account names into the debit or credit column of the trial balance.**
- **Totalling both columns of the trial balance**

Do not enter figures with decimal places in this task and do not enter a zero in unused column cells.

Salaries

Date 20XX	Details	Amount £	Date 20XX	Details	Amount £
30 Jun	Balance b/f	4,537			
30 Jun	Bank	2,901	30 Jun	Balance c/d	7,438
		7,438			7,438

Purchases ledger control account

Date 20XX	Details	Amount £	Date 20XX	Details	Amount £
			1 Jun	Balance b/f	29,389
30 Jun	Balance c/d	35,267	30 Jun	Purchases	5,878
		35,267			35,267

Account name	Amount £	Debit £	Credit £
Salaries			
Purchases ledger control			
Bank	9,267		
Capital	1,000		
Discounts allowed	1,004		
Discounts received	2,940		
Motor vehicles	15,000		
Administration expenses	5,903		
Purchases	89,262		
Sales	90,326		
Sales ledger control	11,892		
Inventory	16,006		
VAT (owing to HM Revenue & Customs)			
Totals			

Task 10

Mandarin Ltd allocates a customer account code to each customer in the sales ledger, as shown below. The code is made up of the first two letters of the customer's name, followed by a number allocated to each customer in that alphabetical group.

Customer name	Customer account code
Dapple Ltd	DA01
Gadabout UK plc	GA01
Grundy Ltd	GR02
Indigo & Co	IN01
Ibber Ltd	IB02
New Aim Ltd	NE01
Roughtrap Ltd	RO01

The two new customer accounts shown below have been added to the sales ledger and need to be allocated a customer account code.

(a) Insert the relevant account codes for each customer.

Doddle plc   Account code: [   ]   Marrion Ltd   Account code: [   ]

Date 20XX	Details	Amount £	Date 20XX	Details	Amount £	Date 20XX	Details	Amount £	Date 20XX	Details	Amount £
3 Aug	Inv 83	532				3 Aug	Inv 91	876			

Mandarin Ltd codes all purchase invoices with a general ledger code. A selection of the codes used is given below.

Item	General Ledger Code
Men's shirts	GL001
Men's trousers	GL002
Women's tops	GL003
Women's trousers	GL004
Sundry clothing	GL005

This is an invoice received from a supplier.

New Aim Ltd 35 Didcot Road, Cinnadon CN7 3DD VAT Registration No. 356 2368 302	
Mandarin Ltd Mandarin House 25 Jedward Street Cinnadon CN6 6LW	
23 July 20XX	
30 womens trousers (product code WT673) @ £16 each	£480.00
VAT @ 20%	£96.00
Total	£576.00

(b) Select which code would be used to code this invoice.

General ledger code	▼

Picklist:

GL001
GL002
GL003
GL004
GL005

(c) Show whether each transaction will be classified as capital expenditure, capital income, revenue expenditure or revenue income by placing the appropriate classification against each transaction in the table below. You can use each classification more than once.

Transaction	Classification
Receipt from sale of a motor vehicle	
Purchase on credit of clothing for resale	
Sale of clothing with one month to pay	
Purchase of shop fittings	
Sale in the factory shop with payment by debit card	
Payment to supplier with one month credit taken	

Classification:

Capital expenditure

Capital income

Revenue expenditure

Revenue income

The business has the following assets and liabilities.

Assets and liabilities	£
Property	35,000
Cash at bank (overdraft)	2,005
Motor Vehicles	15,435
Inventories	3,780
VAT owed to HMRC	22,446
Amounts owing from credit customers	11,223

(d) **Show the accounting equation by inserting the appropriate figures.**

Assets £	Liabilities £	Capital £

(e) **For each of the items below, identify an example from the picklist provided.**

Item	Example
Asset	▼
Liability	▼
Capital transaction	▼

Picklist:

Contribution from owners
Petty cash
Trade payables

BPP PRACTICE ASSESSMENT 4
Bookkeeping Transactions

ANSWERS

Bookkeeping Transactions
BPP practice assessment 4

Task 1

(a)

Mandarin Ltd Mandarin House, 25 Jedward Street Cinnadon CN6 6LW					

VAT Registration No. 928 2781 110

CREDIT NOTE

Jessop Brothers Unit 10 Eastern Trading Estate Cinnadon CN1 1PP	Customer account code: SL930
Credit note number no: CN01256 Delivery note number: 452634 Order number: 876238	Date: 22 July 20XX

Quantity of goods	Product code	Total list price £	Net amount after discount £	VAT £	Gross £
20	WT555	120.00	108.00	21.60	129.60

Tutorial note. Workings: List price 20 × £30/5 = £120, net after trade discount = £120 × 90% = £108, VAT = £108 × 20% = £21.60

(b) Sales returns daybook

Date 20XX	Details	Credit note number	Total £	VAT £	Net £
22 Jul	Jessop Brothers	CN01256	129.60	21.60	108.00

(c)

Mandarin Ltd Mandarin House 25 Jedward Street Cinnadon CN6 6LW		
To: Tarsus & Co	Date: 31 July 20XX	
Date 20XX and details	**Transaction amount** **£**	**Outstanding amount** **£**
21 July – Invoice 01250	324	324
22 July – Credit note 013	12	312
30 July – Invoice 01301	1,285	1,597
31 July – Cheque	302	1,295
31 July – Discount taken	10	1,285

(d) The correct answer is: sales invoice 0102

(e) The correct answer is: £2,918.40

Working:

Gross amount before discount: £2,560.00 + (£2,560.00 × 20%) = £3,072.00

After discount: £3,072.00 × 95% = £2,918.40

Task 2

(a)

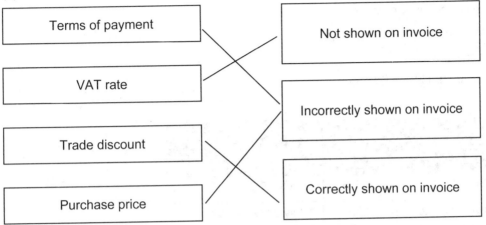

Terms of payment	Not shown on invoice
VAT rate	Incorrectly shown on invoice
Trade discount	
Purchase price	Correctly shown on invoice

(b)

	Yes ✓	No ✓
What would be the VAT amount charged if the invoice was correct?	£	51.84
What would be the total amount charged if the invoice was correct?	£	311.04

Tutorial note.

Purchase price: 40 × £36/5 = £288
Price after discount: £288 × 90% = £259.20
VAT: £259.20 × 20% = £51.84
Total: £259.20 + £51.84 = £311.04

(c)

Purchases day book

Date 20XX	Details	Invoice number	Total £	VAT £	Net £	Women's clothing £	Men's clothing £
30 Jun	Forfar Textiles plc	C9230	1,872	312	1,560		1,560
30 Jun	Jessamy Fashion Inc	0024567	3,216	536	2,680	2,680	
30 Jun	Lindstrom Ltd	726	3,888	648	3,240	3,240	
	Totals		8,976	1,496	7,480	5,920	1,560

Task 3

(a) The correct answer is: payment for £3,205

(b) The correct answer is: credit note C98

(c) The correct answer is: £2,585

Working

£5,790 – £3,205 = £2,585

(d)

Supplier	£	Date by which payment should be received by supplier
Bumble plc	4,455	13 July 20XX
Hallidays Ltd	2,850	9 July 20XX

Tutorial note.

Bumble plc: £4,500 × 99% = £4,455

Hallidays Ltd: £3,000 × 95% = £2,850

Task 4

(a) Cash book – debit side

Details	Cash £	Bank £	VAT £	Trade receivables £	Cash sales £
Balance b/f	1,869				
Vampeter Ltd		1,256		1,256	
Propos Co	900		150		750
Total	2,769	1,256	150	1,256	750

(b) Cash book – credit side

Details	Cash £	Bank £	VAT £	Trade payables £	Cash purchases £	Office expenses £
Balance b/f		1,249				
Diston Ltd		4,295		4,295		
Opra Office Supplies		336	56			280
Total		5,880	56	4,295		280

(c) The correct answer is: £2,769

(d) The correct answer is: -£4,624 (£1,256 – £5,880 = -£4,624)

(e) The correct answer is: Credit

Task 5

(a) Petty cash book

Details	Amount £	Details	Amount £	VAT £	Entertainment £	Travel £
Balance b/f	100.00	Harry's Café	26.30		26.30	
		Tune Travel	38.88	6.48		32.40
		Balance c/d	34.82			
Total	100.00	Totals	100.00	6.48	26.30	32.40

(b) General ledger

Account name	Amount £	Debit ✓	Credit ✓
Petty cash control	92.76		✓
Motor expenses	42.80	✓	
Sundry expenses	22.78	✓	
Postage	17.26	✓	
VAT	9.92	✓	

Task 6

(a) Rupert Reynolds

Details	£	Details	£
		Discount allowed	33

(b)

Discounts received

Details	£	Details	£
		Purchases ledger control	635

VAT

Details	£	Details	£
		Purchases ledger control	127

Purchases ledger control

Details	£	Details	£
Discounts received	635		
VAT	127		

Task 7

(a) Sales ledger

Account name	Amount £	Debit ✓	Credit ✓
Singer & Co	1,934		✓

(b) General ledger

Account name	Amount £	Debit ✓	Credit ✓
Sales ledger control	1,934		✓
Cash sales	630		✓
VAT	126		✓

Task 8

(a)

Motor expenses

Date 20XX	Details	Amount £	Date 20XX	Details	Amount £
01 Jun	Balance b/d	2,904			
15 Jun	Purchases ledger control	276			
30 Jun	Purchases ledger control	184			
			30 Jun	Balance c/d	3,364
	Total	3,364		Total	3,364
1 Jul	Balance b/d	3,364			

Discounts received

Date 20XX	Details	Amount £	Date 20XX	Details	Amount £
			01 Jun	Balance b/d	926
			15 Jun	Purchases ledger control	64
			30 Jun	Purchases ledger control	25
30 Jun	Balance c/d	1,015			
	Total	1,015		Total	1,015
			1 Jul	Balance b/d	1,015

Task 9

Account name	Amount £	Debit £	Credit £
Salaries		7,438	
Purchases ledger control			35,267
Bank	9,267	9,267	
Capital	1,000		1,000
Discounts allowed	1,004	1,004	
Discounts received	2,940		2,940
Motor vehicles	15,000	15,000	
Administration expenses	5,903	5,903	
Purchases	89,262	89,262	
Sales	90,326		90,326
Sales ledger control	11,892		11,892
Inventory	16,006	16,006	
VAT (owing to HM Revenue & Customs)			2,455
Totals		143,880	143,880

Task 10

(a) **Doddle plc Account code:** | DO02 |

Marrion Ltd Account code: | MA01 |

(b)

| General ledger code | GL004 |

(c)

Transaction	Classification
Receipt from sale of a motor vehicle	Capital income
Purchase on credit of clothing for resale	Revenue expenditure
Sale of clothing with one month to pay	Revenue income
Purchase of shop fittings	Capital expenditure
Sale in the factory shop with payment by debit card	Revenue income
Payment to supplier with one month credit taken	Revenue expenditure

(d)

Assets £	Liabilities £	Capital £
65,438	24,451	40,987

Tutorial note.

Assets = £35,000 + £15,435 + £3,780 + £11,223 = £65,438

Liabilities = £2,005 + £22,446 = £24,451

Capital = Assets – Liabilities = £65,438 – £24,451 = £40,987

(e)

Item	Example
Asset	Petty cash
Liability	Trade payables
Capital transaction	Contribution from owners

Notes

Notes

Notes

Notes

Notes